P9-CEV-721

Understanding American History

The Abolition of Slavery

Diane Yancey

Bruno Leone
Series Consultant

ReferencePoint Press®

San Diego, CA

© 2013 ReferencePoint Press, Inc.
Printed in the United States

For more information, contact:
ReferencePoint Press, Inc.
PO Box 27779
San Diego, CA 92198
www.ReferencePointPress.com

ALL RIGHTS RESERVED.
No part of this work covered by the copyright hereon may be reproduced or used in any form or by any means—graphic, electronic, or mechanical, including photocopying, recording, taping, web distribution, or information storage retrieval systems—without the written permission of the publisher.

LIBRARY OF CONGRESS CATALOGING-IN-PUBLICATION DATA

Yancey, Diane.
  The abolition of slavery / by Diane Yancey.
     p. cm. -- (Understanding American history series)
  Includes bibliographical references and index.
  ISBN-13: 978-1-60152-476-8 (hardback)
  ISBN-10: 1-60152-476-5 (hardback)
  1. Antislavery movements--United States--History--19th century--Juvenile literature.
  2. Abolitionists--United States--History--19th century--Juvenile literature. I. Title.
  E449.Y36 2013
  326'.80973--dc23
                                                                    2012005992

Contents

Foreword

America's Puritan ancestors—convinced that their adopted country was blessed by God and would eventually rise to worldwide prominence—proclaimed their new homeland the shining "city upon a hill." The nation that developed since those first hopeful words were uttered has clearly achieved prominence on the world stage and it has had many shining moments but its history is not without flaws. The history of the United States is a virtual patchwork of achievements and blemishes. For example, America was originally founded as a New World haven from the tyranny and persecution prevalent in many parts of the Old World. Yet the colonial and federal governments in America took little or no action against the use of slave labor by the southern states until the 1860s, when a civil war was fought to eliminate slavery and preserve the federal union.

In the decades before and after the Civil War, the United States underwent a period of massive territorial expansion; through a combination of purchase, annexation, and war, its east–west borders stretched from the Atlantic to the Pacific Oceans. During this time, the Industrial Revolution that began in eighteenth-century Europe found its way to America, where it was responsible for considerable growth of the national economy. The United States was now proudly able to take its place in the Western Hemisphere's community of nations as a worthy economic and technological partner. Yet America also chose to join the major western European powers in a race to acquire colonial empires in Africa, Asia, and the islands of the Caribbean and South Pacific. In this scramble for empire, foreign territories were often peacefully annexed but military force was readily used when needed, as in the Philippines during the Spanish-American War of 1898.

Toward the end of the nineteenth century and concurrent with America's ambitions to acquire colonies, its vast frontier and expanding industrial base provided both land and jobs for a new and ever-growing wave of immigrants from southern and eastern Europe. Although America had always encouraged immigration, these newcomers—Italians, Greeks, and eastern European Jews, among others—were seen as different from the vast majority of earlier immigrants, most of whom were from northern and western Europe. The presence of these newcomers was treated as a matter of growing concern, which in time evolved into intense opposition. Congress boldly and with calculated prejudice set out to create a barrier to curtail the influx of unwanted nationalities and ethnic groups to America's shores. The outcome was the National Origins Act, passed in 1924. That law severely reduced immigration to the United States from southern and eastern Europe. Ironically, while this was happening, the Statue of Liberty stood in New York Harbor as a visible and symbolic beacon lighting the way for people of *all* nationalities and ethnicities seeking sanctuary in America.

Unquestionably, the history of the United States has not always mirrored that radiant beacon touted by the early settlers. As often happens, reality and dreams tend to move in divergent directions. However, the story of America also reveals a people who have frequently extended a helping hand to a weary world and who have displayed a ready willingness—supported by a flexible federal constitution—to take deliberate and effective steps to correct injustices, past and present. America's private and public philanthropy directed toward other countries during times of natural disasters (such as the contributions of financial and human resources to assist Haiti following the January 2010, earthquake) and the legal right to adopt amendments to the US Constitution (including the Thirteenth Amendment freeing the slaves and the Nineteenth Amendment granting women the right to vote) are examples of the nation's generosity and willingness to acknowledge and reverse wrongs.

With objectivity and candor, the titles selected for the Understanding American History series portray the many sides of America, depicting both its shining moments and its darker hours. The series strives to help readers achieve a wider understanding and appreciation of the American experience and to encourage further investigation into America's evolving character and founding principles.

Important Events During the
Abolition of Slavery

1655
On March 8 John Casor becomes the first person of African descent to be officially declared a slave for life in the American colonies.

1794
On March 14 Eli Whitney patents his new invention, the cotton gin.

1850
Between September 9 and 20, the Fugitive Slave Act and the Compromise of 1850 become law.

| 1650 | 1795 | 1815 | 1835 | 1855 |

1775
On April 14 the first abolition society, the Pennsylvania Society for Promoting the Abolition of Slavery, is created in America.

1820
On March 3 Congress passes the Missouri Compromise.

1852
On March 20 Harriet Beecher Stowe's book *Uncle Tom's Cabin* is published.

1854
On May 30 the Kansas-Nebraska Act, which effectively repeals the Missouri Compromise, becomes law.

1860
On November 6 Abraham Lincoln is elected president of the United States.

1957
On February 14 the Southern Christian Leadership Conference (SCLC) is created.

1863
On January 1 Lincoln's Emancipation Proclamation effectively abolishes slavery in the United States.

1955
On December 1 Rosa Parks's act of civil disobedience in Montgomery, Alabama, marks the beginning of the civil rights movement.

1963
On August 28 the March on Washington for Jobs and Freedom takes place.

1877
On May 1 Reconstruction comes to an end when President Rutherford B. Hayes orders the removal of US troops from the South.

1968
On April 4 Martin Luther King Jr. is assassinated.

1860   1890   1900   1950   2000

1896
On May 18 in *Plessy v. Ferguson* the Supreme Court legitimizes segregation under the separate but equal doctrine.

2008
On November 4 Barack Obama is elected the first African American president of the United States.

1865
On April 9 the Civil War ends and the Reconstruction Era begins.

1867
On February 14 as a result of his quarrel with Congress over Reconstruction, President Andrew Johnson becomes the first US president to be impeached.

1861
On April 12 the Civil War begins.

1964
On July 2 President Lyndon Johnson passes the Civil Rights Act of 1964.

The Defining Characteristics of the Abolition of Slavery

On July 4, 1829, 24-year-old editor and activist William Lloyd Garrison stepped in front of a group of Bostonians who had gathered in Park Street Church to celebrate Independence Day. In a speech with the theme "Dangers to the Nation," the bespectacled Garrison spoke on a topic that was of growing interest to Americans—the evils of slavery and the need to abolish it.

It was Garrison's first public address, but his words were passionate and uncompromising. He declared that slavery—the practice of holding people in bondage against their will—was immoral and unjustifiable. He pointed out that slaveholders and non-slaveholders alike were guilty; the former because they practiced it, and the latter because they did not assist in overthrowing it. He argued that America, a country that stood for freedom and equality, should be embarassed by its hypocrisy. "Every Fourth of July, our Declaration of Independence is produced . . . to set forth the tyranny of the mother country (England) and to challenge the admiration of the world. But what a pitiful detail of grievances does this document present, in comparison with the wrongs which our slaves endure! . . . I am ashamed of my country!"[1]

Garrison not only pressed for immediate nationwide emancipation, he went so far as to propose that free states break away from slaveholding states if they would not agree to abolition. "This monstrous inequality [slavery] should no longer be tolerated. If it cannot be speedily put down—not by force but by fair persuasion, . . . if we must share in the guilt and danger of destroying the bodies and souls of men, *as the price of our Union*, . . . then the fault is not ours if a separation eventually takes place."[2]

Deeply Divided

Garrison's address was a sign of the strong feelings that slavery had begun to stir up in America in the 1800s. As opponents of the practice became more outspoken and critical, conflict and division grew.

Residents of Southern states such as South Carolina, Virginia, and Louisiana saw slavery as an American right and a necessity for survival.

Black slaves work in a sweet potato field on a South Carolina plantation in 1862. The agricultural economy of the South depended on the free labor of thousands of slaves who planted, tended, and harvested crops.

Their economies were based on growing crops like cotton, tobacco, and rice. Thousands of slaves were necessary to plant, tend, and harvest the fields. Freeing them meant giving up a great deal of wealth as well as future prosperity. This was unthinkable, and those who owned or relied on slaves were willing to fight to keep their property and their way of life. Southern statesman John C. Calhoun wrote in February of 1837, "If we concede an inch, concession would follow concession—compromise would follow compromise, until our ranks would be so broken that effectual resistance would be impossible. We must meet the enemy on the frontier, with a fixed determination of maintaining our position at every hazard. . . . We of the South will not, cannot, surrender our institutions."[3]

In the North, the economy was industrial, so Northerners did not rely on slaves for their prosperity. All Northern states had abolished or were abolishing slavery by 1804. Some Northerners were motivated by idealism—the belief that slavery was immoral—but for those of the working classes the motive was more practical. They did not want slaves working at jobs where whites could otherwise earn a living. Historian Edgar McManus writes, "Whites of the working class . . . feared the free Negro as an economic competitor. They supported emancipation not to raise the Negro to a better life but to destroy a system which gave him a fixed place in the economy."[4]

A Rare Combination of Circumstances

Despite the fact that slavery had been an issue in America since its creation, it was not abolished nationwide until the 1860s. At that time a unique combination of people and events came together under circumstances that aggravated the long-term conflict and made emancipation not only possible but unavoidable.

Some of the people were abolitionists, men and women willing to step forward, speak out, fight, and even die to end slavery throughout the United States. They included Garrison, former slave Frederick Douglass, and Henry Ward Beecher, who agitated in public meetings and in articles published far and wide. The abolitionists worked to change

A Conflicted Society

Proslavery Americans argued that slavery dated far back in history. In "Interview with James O. Horton," the historian explains that American slavery was distinctive, however, because it was based on race.

> It's important to realize that slavery is not an American invention. Slavery is as old as recorded human society. In fact, we realize that the English word "slave," comes from the word "Slav," and it was applied to those people in eastern Europe who were bound and brought to the Mediterranean where they grew sugar. The fact is that slavery is a very old institution—there was slavery in various parts of Europe, and in various parts of Africa.
>
> But the thing that makes American slavery so distinctive is it is based on race. America's slavery is justified not, for example, as West African slavery is justified—where people were captured in battle and then held in a kind of captivity. Think about that for a second. Any of us could have lost that battle. Any of us could have been held in captivity. Any of us could have been a slave. But when you base slavery on the question of race, then if one of us is black and one is white and slavery is linked to blackness, then one of us could never have been a slave.

PBS, "Interview with James O. Horton," *RACE—The Power of an Illusion*, 2003. www.pbs.org.

laws to stop slavery's spread. They helped slaves escape to freedom. They were motivated by the belief that the immoral institution could not be excused or permitted to endure a moment longer than was necessary. As Garrison, one of the most outspoken abolitionists, said, "On

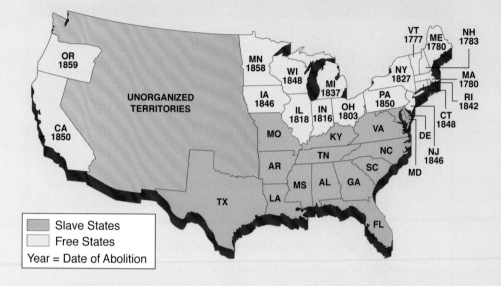

Slave and Free States Circa 1860

OR 1859

UNORGANIZED TERRITORIES

CA 1850

MN 1858

WI 1848

IA 1846

MO

MI 1837

IL 1818

IN 1816

OH 1803

KY

TN

AR

MS

AL

GA

TX

LA

FL

VT 1777

ME 1780

NH 1783

NY 1827

MA 1780

PA 1850

RI 1842

CT 1848

VA

DE

NC

NJ 1846

SC

MD

Slave States
Free States
Year = Date of Abolition

this subject I do not wish to think, or speak, or write with moderation. . . . I am in earnest—I will not equivocate [avoid the issue]—I will not excuse—I will not retreat a single inch—and I will be heard."[5]

Significant events also played a role in making slavery a crisis issue in the mid-1800s. As the nation expanded to the south and west, the rights of slaveholders who wanted to settle the new territories clashed with those who wanted the new lands to be free. Laws that aimed to settle the debates merely inflamed one side or the other. By the 1850s, tempers ran high every time slavery or its abolition was mentioned. Abolitionists became more forceful in their demands, and Southerners laid plans for dealing with the government should it outlaw slavery.

Conflict Leads to War

Eventually, the conflict boiled over into civil war, during which time both sides took unwavering stands from which there was no turning back. In 1861, 11 states seceded from the United States and formed the Confederate States of America. The Confederacy's vice president Alexander H. Stephens declared, "Our new government is founded on the opposite idea of the equality of the races. . . . Its corner stone rests upon the great truth that the Negro is not equal to the white man. This . . . government is the first in the history of the world, based upon this great physical and moral truth."[6]

The North opposed slavery, but its stand was based on the need to preserve the Union. The United States had been created with great sacrifice less than 100 years before, and the thought of its failing as a nation was unthinkable. As President Abraham Lincoln wrote to *New York Tribune* editor Horace Greeley in 1862, "My paramount object in this struggle *is* to save the Union, and is *not* either to save or to destroy slavery. If I could save the Union without freeing *any* slave I would do it, and if I could save it by freeing *all* the slaves I would do it; and if I could save it by freeing some and leaving others alone I would also do that."[7] A combination of circumstances, however, eventually worked to change Lincoln's priorities. Historian Barbara J. Fields writes, "The government discovered that it could not accomplish its narrow goal—union—without adopting the slaves' nobler one—universal emancipation."[8]

By the time the war ended, slavery had been abolished. The end of slavery, however, did not end the conflict and division that had swirled around the issue. Americans in the North and South continued to have different points of view over the status of blacks in America. Violence erupted time and again as both sides struggled to achieve their different and often opposite goals. And everyone knew that the problem was not liable to be easily solved. Disputes over slavery went back to the colonization of the country. It would take centuries of work to accomplish what emancipation had only begun in 1865.

Chapter 1

What Conditions Led to the Abolition of Slavery?

Two basic conditions led to the abolition of slavery in the United States. The first was the presence of slaves and slaveholders. The former arrived in 1619, when a Dutch ship docked at the port of Jamestown, Virginia, carrying 20 Africans who were traded to English colonists in return for food and supplies. These captives were technically known as indentured servants, which meant they were owned by their masters for a period of time and then freed. Other captives from Africa soon followed, and by the end of the century, English colonists were purposefully importing slaves to satisfy their desire for cheap labor. An estimated 645,000 Africans were carried to the United States before 1800. Until 1777, slavery was legal in all of the 13 original states.

The second condition that led to the abolition of slavery was the presence of men and women who saw the practice as wrong and wanted to end it. Originally, most of these were German and Dutch Quakers (Society of Friends) in Pennsylvania, whose religious stand against violence and injustice made slavery morally wrong. They published a condemnation of the practice in 1688: "There is a saying that we shall doe to all men like as we will be done ourselves; making no difference of what generation, descent or colour they are. . . . To bring men hither, or to rob and sell them against their will, we stand against."[9]

Early Abolition Societies

The Quakers' forceful arguments against slavery eventually led to banning the practice within the Society of Friends. The Quakers also formed the first American abolition society in April 1776. It was called the Society for the Relief of Free Negroes Unlawfully Held in Bondage (soon renamed the Pennsylvania Society for Promoting the Abolition of Slavery). Its first president was Benjamin Franklin. Franklin himself owned two slaves, and he originally believed that blacks were inferior to whites. He came to question his beliefs, however, after visiting a school where young African Americans proved that they were capable of being educated. In February 1790 he petitioned the US Senate and House of Representatives on behalf of the Pennsylvania Society, stating, "[We] earnestly entreat your serious attention to the Subject of Slavery, that you will be pleased to countenance the Restoration of liberty to those unhappy Men, who alone, in this land of Freedom, are degraded into perpetual Bondage."[10]

Demands by Americans to end slavery were temporarily set aside during the Revolutionary War, which raged from 1775 to 1783. Upon declaring themselves free from Britain in 1776, however, the new country's leaders clearly stated their belief in the equality of all men in the Declaration of Independence. It states: "We hold these truths to be self-evident, that all men are created equal, and that they are endowed by their Creator with certain unalienable Rights, that among these are Life, Liberty and the pursuit of Happiness."[11]

One of the founding fathers, John Jay, felt so strongly about the equality of men that he established another early abolition society, the New York Manumission Society, after the war in 1785. Jay, the society's first president, also persuaded statesmen Alexander Hamilton and Aaron Burr to join. The society organized boycotts against merchants in the slave trade and newspapers that supported that trade. It also provided legal counsel for free blacks—blacks who had been emancipated or had never been slaves—who had been claimed as slaves. It also helped pass the Act for Gradual Abolition of Slavery in New York State in 1799.

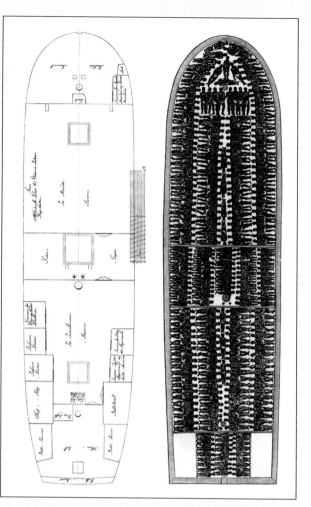

Slave traders packed their ships with African captives who would be sold as slaves upon reaching the American colonies. A hand-colored woodcut of a slave-trading ship from the 1700s depicts the wretched conditions of the journey.

Compromise and the Constitution

Early abolitionists could not drown out the voices of the slavery supporters, however. These men and women believed slavery was necessary for the good of the country, particularly the South. Landowners there benefited from free field labor to raise tobacco and cotton. Without slaves, all of those crops would be less profitable, and the Southern economy would decline.

In 1787, when 55 delegates met to create the constitution of the newly formed United States and to spell out the rights of its citizens, some of the most powerful slaveholders in the country were present. It soon became clear that these men might refuse to take part in the convention if slavery were outlawed. One participant, statesman James Madison wrote, "It seems now to be pretty well understood that the real difference of interests lies . . . between the northern and southern states. The institution of slavery and its consequences form the line of discrimination."[12]

Arguments over the issue were passionate, and there seemed to be no good solution. If slavery continued, slaves would suffer. If it were abolished, the new nation's shaky economy could be hurt. Thomas Jefferson colorfully described the country's predicament: "We have the wolf by the ear, and we can neither hold him, nor safely let him go. Justice is in one scale, and self-preservation in the other."[13]

The Difficulty of Compromise

Although it was difficult, members of the Constitutional Convention eventually agreed to compromise. They decided that slavery would not be abolished nationwide, although no mention of the words "slave" or "slavery" was made in the Constitution itself. Instead, states would be allowed to decide whether they would allow the practice or not. The slave trade would end on January 1, 1808. That meant that no new slaves would be imported into the United States after that date. States would be represented in the House of Representatives according to population, but a slave would count as only three-fifths of a white person in the census. Though this seems insulting to slaves as humans, in fact it prevented Southern states with large slave populations from having unfair influence in Congress.

As time passed, the compromise proved difficult to live with. The country grew, new slave and free states were added to the Union, and maintaining equal representation in Congress proved tricky. The issue was avoided for a time because for each slave state that entered the Union, a free state entered as well. But no one could guarantee that this balance could continue indefinitely.

A solution would definitely be needed at some point because the philosophies of the two parts of the country—North and South—were becoming more widely divided and more hostile all the time. The North was developing into a fast-paced manufacturing society that was happy to rely on a central government to direct its future. The South remained agricultural. Southerners clung to an unhurried way of life supported by slaves, and they gave their loyalty to a single state more than to the Union. French political thinker and historian Alexis de Tocqueville emphasized the tension this produced.

> Every day (the North) grows more wealthy and densely populated while the South is stationary or growing poor. . . . The [result] . . . is a violent change in the equilibrium of power and political influence. Powerful states become weak, territories without a name become states. . . . Wealth, like population, is displaced. These changes cannot take place without injuring interest, without exciting passions.[14]

Arguments for Slavery

As tension over the future of slavery heightened, both sides brought arguments to support their positions. Proslavery adherents believed that the federal government had no right to dictate to the states what their policies should be. They cited Jefferson, who had written in 1798 that the states had the right of self-government and did not owe unlimited submission to the federal government. Jefferson had stated, "Whensoever the general government assumes undelegated powers, its acts are unauthoritative, void, and of no force."[15]

There were also Southerners such as South Carolina statesman John C. Calhoun who argued that slavery was "a positive good"[16] because slaves in America experienced a higher standard of living than they ordinarily would in Africa. There they had lived in primitive conditions, had not been able to associate with "civilized" people (meaning people of European background), and had not been exposed to Western culture, education, medicine, and the like. Calhoun said, "Never before has the black race of Central Africa, from the dawn of history to the present day, attained a condition so civilized and so improved, not only physically, but morally and intellectually."[17]

America's First Slave

The first official slave owner in North America was a black man named Anthony Johnson, who had been an indentured servant when he arrived in Virginia in 1621. An indentured servant was essentially a slave who was owned for five to seven years, worked for a master for no pay, but then was freed. There were no official slaves in America at the time.

By July 1651 Johnson had been freed and had five indentured servants of his own. One of the servants, John Casor, went to court, claiming that Johnson had held him past his term of service. Unexpectedly, the court sided against Casor, stating that Johnson could own him for life. In 1655 Casor thus became the first recognized slave for life in the colony of Virginia and the future United States.

Calhoun and others also believed that slavery was good because it introduced slaves to Christianity and saved their souls. Many slave owners also believed they were protectors of their slaves, whom they considered mentally incapable of living on their own. If slaves were not supervised and guided throughout their lives, slave owners rationalized, they would be like little children, destitute and afraid. Author William G. Eliot wrote of one slave owner's wife in 1863, "She felt deeply through her whole nature, as most of the well-born Southern women did, that there was a trust involved for which the slave-owner was responsible to God almost as sacredly as for his own children."[18]

More Arguments

Slaveholders not only held that slavery was good for America, they also argued that it was a commonly accepted practice of humankind. They pointed out that it had existed throughout history—the ancient Greeks and Romans had slaves. In the Bible, Old Testament patriarch Abraham had slaves, and in the New Testament, the apostle Paul, a Christian, had returned a runaway slave, Philemon, to his master.

Despite all the rationalizing, slaveholders' fundamental reason for keeping slaves was economic. By 1860 almost half of the states in the United States—15 out of 33—relied on slaves for free manual labor. Few slave owners would have been able to afford to pay laborers to do the work that slaves did for nothing. Likewise, Southern coal mines, tanneries, ironworks, textile mills, and tobacco factories that relied heavily on slave labor would not have been as profitable for their owners if they had had to pay wages. Without slave labor, many farms and businesses would have failed.

Not only did slaves help plantations and businesses thrive, slave owners had a great deal of money invested in the slaves themselves. A healthy field hand was worth an average of $400 to $600 in the United States in 1800, and most slaveholders owned several. By 1850 a slave was worth between $1,300 and $1,500. By 1860 that figure had risen to $3,000. For plantation owners who owned 20 or more slaves, the value of their human property was sometimes more than the value of their land and implements combined. Freeing their slaves and losing such large sums of money was unthinkable to them.

The Cotton Gin

Slaves had always been important to Southern society, but they became indispensable after the invention of the mechanical cotton gin in 1793. Prior to that time, cotton fibers were separated from the seeds by hand, a time-consuming process that limited cotton production. When inventor Eli Whitney came up with the idea of using slender metal spikes to comb the seeds out of fiber, a single mechanical gin could clean 50 pounds (22.7kg) of lint per day. Cotton production expanded from 750,000 bales in 1830 to 2.85 million bales in 1850. By 1860 the South was providing 80 percent of Great Britain's cotton and two-thirds of the world's supply of cotton. Senator James Henry Hammond

Slaves use a cotton gin to clean seeds from cotton fiber. Cotton production, and the need for slave labor, increased dramatically with the invention of the mechanical cotton gin.

of South Carolina declared in 1858: "What would happen if no cotton was furnished for three years? England would topple headlong and carry the whole civilized world with her."[19]

As the ability to plant, tend, and harvest greater amounts of cotton increased, the number of slaves increased in the South, too. Between the first federal census in 1790 and the eve of the Civil War, the slave population in the United States grew from approximately 700,000 to almost 4 million.

By 1860 one in three Southerners was a slave. There were over 2 million slaves in the lower Southern states (Texas, Alabama, Georgia, Louisiana, Mississippi, South Carolina, and Florida), and over 1 million in the upper South (Virginia, Tennessee, North Carolina, and Arkansas). Almost half a million more slaves resided in the border states of Kentucky, Missouri, Maryland, Delaware, as well as the District of Columbia.

The Mudsill Theory

Many proslavery men such as James Henry Hammond justified their belief in slavery by stating that slaves were the "mudsill" of society. A mudsill is the lowest timber supporting a building at ground level. Hammond explained his theory in a speech to the US Senate on March 4, 1858.

> In all social systems there must be a class to do the menial duties, to perform the drudgery of life. That is, a class requiring but a low order of intellect and but little skill. Its requisites are vigor, docility, fidelity [energy, submissiveness, faithfulness]. Such a class you must have, or you would not have that other class which leads progress, civilization, and refinement. It constitutes the very mud-sill of society and of political government; and you might as well attempt to build a house in the air, as to build either the one or the other, except on this mud-sill. Fortunately for the South, she found a race adapted to that purpose to her hand. A race inferior to her own, but eminently qualified in temper, in vigor, in docility, in capacity to stand the climate, to answer all her purposes. We use them for our purpose, and call them slaves.

PBS, "The 'Mudsill Theory' by James Henry Hammond," *Africans in America*, 1998. www.pbs.org.

Quality of Life

Many slaves in the South lived on plantations—large farms or estates where crops were grown on vast stretches of land. Slaveholders insisted that slaves were well cared for, but in fact their lives were miserable. Freedman and abolitionist Jermaine Wesley Loguen wrote of the hopelessness most felt: "No day ever dawns for the slave, nor it is looked for. For the slave it is all night—all night, forever."[20]

Most slaves lived in one-room, dirt-floored shacks that were located well away from the owner's home. The shacks were drafty, had gaping holes in the walls, roofs that leaked, and chimneys that often caught fire. Although small, they commonly housed up to a dozen men, women, and children. Residents cooked over open fires and slept on the ground on mattresses filled with corn husks. For meals, the women used cornmeal, molasses, salt, and a few other basics provided by the plantation owner, but any meat or vegetables had to be provided by slaves themselves. Slave families grew or gathered their food only after they had finished their day's work for their masters. Former slave William Moore recalls, "We had a purty hard time to make out and was hongry lots of times. Marse [Master] Tom didn't feel called on to feed his hands any too much. I 'members I had a cravin' for victuals [food] all the time."[21]

Because of overcrowded, dirty conditions, illnesses such as pneumonia, cholera, and tuberculosis were common, and the death rate for children and the elderly was high. At least 20 percent of slave children died before the age of five. While it was in the economic interest of planters to keep their slaves healthy, most did not provide satisfactory medical care, and slaves regularly suffered from tooth decay, worms, and dysentery.

Hard Work and Fear

While dealing with bad living conditions and poor health, slaves were expected to work long and hard beginning at an early age. When they were four, they could work as babysitters. Around the age of five, they would be assigned to run errands and carry water. Around the age of eight, they were put to work beside their parents in the field. Former slave Sarah Frances Shaw Graves remembers, "I carried water for field hands. I've carried three big buckets of water from one field to another, from one place to another; one in each hand and one balanced on my head."[22]

House servants were on call any time of day or night. Field hands worked from dawn to late into the night if there was a full moon. An unidentified slave owner wrote in 1850, "It is expected that (slaves) should rise early enough to be at work by the time it is light. . . . While at work they should be brisk. . . . I have no objection to their whistling or singing some lively tune, but no drawling [slow] tunes are allowed . . . for their motions are almost certain to keep time with the music."[23]

Slaves also lived in a state of constant fear and uncertainty. If they did not perform up to expectations, they could be whipped or even killed. Even if they performed satisfactorily, they could be sold and moved to another plantation or another state. Families were often torn

The typical slave quarters housed a dozen men, women, and children and consisted of a one-room shack with a dirt floor, leaky roof, and holes in the walls. A photograph from the 1800s shows a group of slaves outside their quarters on a Georgia plantation.

apart at a moment's notice, never to see one another again. Men and women married, but it was understood that not only death but distance would end the relationship. Trying to get an education was also dangerous because owners recognized that knowledge was power. A slave who learned to read might then learn how to escape. "If they caught us with a piece of paper in our pockets, they'd whip us," said one unidentified female slave. "They was afraid we'd learn to read and write, but I never got the chance."[24]

Uncle Tom's Cabin

Despite such inhumane conditions, most Americans tolerated slavery. Southerners believed it was natural and normal for blacks to be enslaved, and few Northerners had ever traveled to the South to see slavery conditions there. In general, they were busy with their own lives and had little time to spend thinking about those whom they believed to be inferior anyway.

All that changed, however, after author Harriet Beecher Stowe published her book *Uncle Tom's Cabin, or Life Among the Lowly* in 1852. She was inspired to write it after reading the 1849 slave narrative *The Life of Josiah Henson, Formerly a Slave, Now an Inhabitant of Canada, as Narrated by Himself*. Henson was a former enslaved black who had lived and worked on a tobacco plantation in Maryland.

Uncle Tom's Cabin centered on a hero, a slave named Uncle Tom, and a villainous slave master, Simon Legree. In the story, Tom's faith in God is tested by the hardships and injustices of slavery, and he eventually sacrifices his life in order to help his friends escape to freedom. The book was fictional, dramatic, and sentimental, but it portrayed the reality of slavery in a powerful way. Its plot and characters educated readers about the issues of racism, slavery, the Fugitive Slave Law, and the future of freed people. Northerners were enthralled and horrified by it. One of Stowe's friends wrote, "I thought I was a thoroughgoing-abolitionist before, but your book has awakened so strong a feeling of indignation and of compassion, that I seem never to have had any feeling on this subject til now."[25]

Two Sides, Two Views

More than 300,000 copies of *Uncle Tom's Cabin* were sold in the United States in the first year. It soon gained fame throughout the world. Letters of praise and appreciation came from England, France, and other countries in Europe. Notables such as Prince Albert of England, vocalist Jenny Lind, and author Charles Dickens thanked Stowe for writing it. Health care pioneer Florence Nightingale wrote regarding her time nursing soldiers in the Crimean War, which lasted from 1853 to 1856, "I hope it may be some pleasure to you . . . to hear that 'Uncle Tom' was read by the sick and suffering in our Eastern Military Hospitals with intense interest."[26]

Stowe and her book were applauded by the public, but they also helped further divide the nation over the issue of slavery. Proslavery forces insisted that Stowe had shown only one side of the practice and that she had exaggerated that side to make it worse than it really was. Abolitionists hailed the work as powerful and inspiring, although some declared it was not a strong enough criticism of the practice. Level-headed leaders worked hard to keep peace between the two sides, but despite their best efforts, the conflict that had characterized the nation since its beginning continued to grow. It would not be long until it flamed into violence that would not be settled except by war.

Chapter 2

Slavery Divides the Nation

Debate and discord between abolitionists and proslavery Americans was stirred up by books like *Uncle Tom's Cabin*, but a series of political decisions between 1820 and 1854 did even more to widen the gap between the two sides. The hatred of one side for the other was so violent by the mid-1800s that Abraham Lincoln spoke for many when he said in 1858: "I believe this government cannot endure, permanently, half slave and half free. . . . Either the opponents of slavery will arrest [stop] the further spread of it and place it where the public mind shall rest in the belief that it is in the course of ultimate extinction, or its advocates will push it forward till it shall become alike lawful in all the states, old as well as new, North as well as South."[27]

Expansion Upsets the Nation's Balance

One of the prime factors that fueled the slavery debate in the 1800s was the westward expansion of the country. This began in 1803, when President Thomas Jefferson decided to purchase 828,000 square miles (2.14 million square km) of land from France. The land known as the Louisiana Purchase lay west of the Mississippi River, ran from the Gulf of Mexico to the Canadian border, and included all or parts of what would eventually become 15 states. There were large slave populations in parts of the purchased area, so Jefferson agreed that slavery would be allowed in the region.

While the decision seemed fair at the time, a problem arose when many more settlers began moving west of the Mississippi River. East of the Mississippi, the Mason-Dixon Line was the accepted boundary between free states in the North and slave states in the South. The line had been created in about 1767 as the result of a boundary dispute between Pennsylvania and Maryland, and it ran between those two states, cut through part of Virginia, and marked the north-south boundary between Maryland and Delaware. Slavery had been contained by the boundary, but west of the Mississippi, no boundary existed. Potentially any territory north or south could become a slave state, a possibility that deeply troubled abolitionists.

Westward expansion also stirred up another troubling issue—the problem of keeping a balance of slave and free states. Up until 1820, the country had had an equal number of each so Congressional and regional power was evenly balanced. Unless two new territories—one slave and one free—applied for statehood at about the same time, however, that balance was liable to be upset. Both North and South grew combative at the thought of the unfair advantage that would result if only one state entered, although both sides regularly pushed for that advantage.

The Missouri Compromise

The Missouri Compromise of 1820 was Congress's response to the problem of Missouri wanting to enter the Union as a result of westward expansion. In 1818 enough settlers had moved into the Missouri Territory for it to apply for statehood. The majority of its residents had come from the Southern United States and had brought along slaves, so it was expected to enter as a slave state. But when the statehood bill was brought before the House of Representatives, James Tallmadge of New York pointed out that it would give the South a representational advantage in Congress. He therefore proposed an amendment that would allow slavery in Missouri but would gradually phase it out. Bringing more slaves into the state would be prohibited, and all blacks born in the state would be given their freedom. Tallmadge declared, "I know the will of my constituents, and regardless of consequences, I will avow it; as their representative, I will proclaim their hatred to slavery in every shape."[28]

Honoring John Brown

Although controversial, John Brown was honored by blacks such as Frederick Douglass. Douglass spoke of Brown's devotion to the antislavery cause in an address at Storer College in West Virginia in 1881.

> His zeal in the cause of my race was far greater than mine—it was as the burning sun to my taper light—mine was bounded by time, his stretched away to the boundless shores of eternity. I could live for the slave, but he could die for him. The crown of martyrdom is high, far beyond the reach of ordinary mortals, and yet happily no special greatness or superior moral excellence is necessary to discern and in some measure appreciate a truly great soul. Cold, calculating and unspiritual as most of us are, we are not wholly insensible to real greatness; and when we are brought in contact with a man of commanding mold, towering high and alone above the millions, free from all conventional fetters, true to his own moral convictions, a "law unto himself," ready to suffer misconstruction, ignoring torture and death for what he believes to be right, we are compelled to do him homage.

Frederick Douglass, "John Brown. An Address at the Fourteenth Anniversary of Storer College, Harper's Ferry, West Virginia, May 30, 1881," Archive.org, 2001. www.archive.org.

Southerners were outraged at Tallmadge's proposal, and although it passed the House of Representatives, it did not pass the Senate. Therefore Missouri remained a territory until 1820, when Maine also applied for statehood as a free state. The issue of Missouri's statehood was then reintroduced, based on the notion that if the two entered at the same time, the balance of slave and free states would remain. Instead of agreeing to the proposal, however, Northern abolitionists in Congress again refused. Their position resulted in heated arguments, name-calling, and threats of secession. The discussions were so violent that Georgia congressman Howell Cobb opined, "A fire has been kindled which all the waters of the ocean cannot put out, and which only seas of blood can extinguish."[29]

Eventually the two sides reached a compromise that passed both houses of Congress but was denounced, in the words of Virginia congressman John Randolph, as "a dirty bargain."[30] Maine and Missouri were admitted as free and slave states respectively. At the same time, an imaginary line was drawn that ran east and west from the Mississippi River to the Pacific Ocean at 36 degrees 30 minutes north latitude (about two thirds of the way down from what is now the northern border of the United States). In the future, states lying north of the line would enter the Union as free, while those south of the line would allow slavery. Missouri remained an exception because it was mostly north of the line but was a slave state.

Further Expansion

The Missouri Compromise, as it became known, remained workable for the next 30 years. Slavery was contained in the South. The admittance of free states Michigan, Wisconsin, and Iowa was balanced by Arkansas, Florida, and Texas coming in as slave states.

In 1848, however, as a result of a war with Mexico, the United States gained another vast amount of territory west of the Louisiana Purchase. That territory included what would become California, Nevada, New Mexico, most of Arizona and Colorado, and parts of Texas, Oklahoma, Kansas, and Wyoming.

Almost before Americans had time to get used to the expansion, gold was discovered in California. In the gold rush of 1849, 300,000 Americans moved to the region, causing the population to grow so rapidly that California was able to apply for statehood in 1850. Its territorial government did not want to allow slavery within its borders, but its land lay both above and below the line of the Missouri Compromise. This caused politicians in Washington, DC, to again argue over slavery—whether the will of Californians should be respected, or whether the territory should be divided into two states, one slave and the other free.

The Compromise of 1850

In September 1850 a compromise was again worked out, although debates were even more heated than previously. At one point the Senate was shocked when Senator Henry S. Foote of Mississippi drew a pistol on Missouri senator Thomas Hart Benton. Benton threw up his hands and shouted, "I have no pistols. Let him fire! Stand out of the way and let the assassin fire!"[31] Despite the excitement, it was finally agreed that the guidelines for the Missouri Compromise would not be applied to land outside the Louisiana Purchase. Instead, when they applied for statehood, settlers in the new territory could determine whether they wanted to be free or slave. Under that rule, California was admitted as a free state.

To help pacify slave-state politicians who had hoped California would be divided, the Fugitive Slave Act of 1850 was also passed in September. It stated that slave owners had the right to hunt down and recapture fugitive slaves even in free states. If slaves resisted or tried to avoid capture, they could be shot and killed. If captured, they could not ask for a jury trial or testify on their own behalf. The act also said that all Northerners had a legal obligation to assist Southerners in the capture of fugitive slaves. Any person caught aiding runaway slaves by providing them food or shelter was subject to six months' imprisonment and a $1,000 fine.

The Fugitive Slave Act, which made Northerners responsible for enforcing slavery even if they morally opposed it, caused enormous anger in the North. Many spoke out against it. An editorial in the *Milwaukee Sentinel* on October 25, 1850, asked, "Is it possible to contemplate these workings of the Fugitive Slave Act with any other feelings than those of shame, disgust and abhorrence?"[32] Some states passed so-called

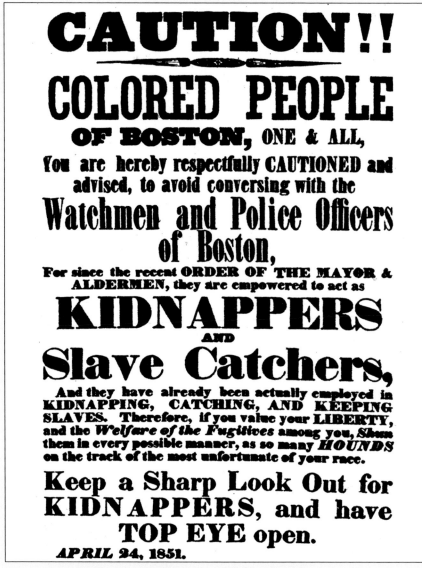

Angered by the Fugitive Slave Act of 1850, which required Northerners to assist Southerners in the capture of fugitive slaves, abolitionists posted signs such as this one urging extreme caution by runaway slaves.

personal liberty laws. These laws combated the act by outlawing the use of state jails to imprison alleged fugitive slaves; by forcing slave hunters to furnish proof that captives were fugitives; and by offering fugitives the right to a jury trial.

Underground Railroad

Other Northerners went further. To combat the act they became part of an underground railroad, a network to help slaves escape into Canada where slavery had been officially abolished in 1834.

The underground railroad was not an actual "railroad" with an engine and cars running on tracks. Instead, it consisted of secret routes, safe houses called stations, and assistance provided by "conductors"—antislavery sympathizers. Conductors came from various backgrounds and included Quakers and members of churches of various denominations. Escaped slaves would travel on foot or by wagon northward along the route from one station to the next.

Slaves usually decided to take the Underground Railroad because of some crisis in their lives. For instance, Henry Brown of Richmond, Virginia, rebelled after his wife and children were sold away from him to a minister who lived hundreds of miles away. In 1849 Brown contacted a member of the Railroad, who packed Brown in a cramped wooden box and shipped him from Richmond to Philadelphia. Brown said of his arrival there: "I had risen as it were from the dead; I felt much more than I could readily express; but as the kindness of Almighty God had been so conspicuously shown in my deliverance, I burst forth into . . . [a hymn] of thanksgiving."[33]

Harriet Tubman

Henry Brown was only one of the daring escapees who used the Underground Railroad. One of the most renowned was former slave Harriet Tubman, nicknamed "Moses" after the biblical patriarch who guided his people to the Promised Land. After escaping and making her way from Maryland to freedom in Philadelphia in 1849, Tubman then became a conductor on the Railroad and personally returned to the South at least 13 times to help her family and others escape.

Tubman was an unlikely heroine. She was a female leader in a male-dominated society. She was not beautiful. She suffered from poor health. After being accidently struck in the head with a heavy weight when she was a teen, she began having headaches and seizures and would lose consciousness. The condition remained with her for her entire life.

Despite such handicaps, Tubman was imaginative and tough, and she relied on these qualities to make her trips successful. For instance, she and her companions would make their escape on a Saturday night, because businesses were closed on Sunday and runaway notices could not be placed in newspapers until Monday morning. If her group met up with possible slave hunters, they would quickly turn around and pretend to be traveling south in order to throw off suspicion. If escapees became too tired or decided to turn back, Tubman pulled out her gun and forced them onward. She knew that if anyone turned back, it could put her and the other escaping slaves in danger of discovery, capture, or even death. "If you hear the dogs, keep going. If you see the torches in the woods, keep going. If there's shouting after you, keep going. Don't ever stop. Keep going. If you want a taste of freedom, keep going,"[34] she said over and over.

Kansas-Nebraska Act

Although the Missouri Compromise had been successfully used for years to deal with Louisiana Purchase territory, political schemes carried out by Congressman Stephen Douglas caused it to be revoked with the passage of the Kansas-Nebraska Act in 1854. Douglas wanted to create the new territories of Kansas and Nebraska to pave the way for building a transcontinental railroad across the nation. Under the Missouri Compromise, both Kansas and Nebraska would have been free states because they were north of the 36 degrees 30 minutes line of latitude. However, Douglas knew that Southern congressmen would not pass the bill unless there was some opportunity for proslavery settlers in the regions. He therefore proposed that, as in the Compromise of 1850, Kansas and Nebraska's territorial governments be allowed to choose whether their territory would be slave or free. He stated, "If the people of Kansas want a slaveholding state let them have it, and if they want a free state they have a right to it."[35]

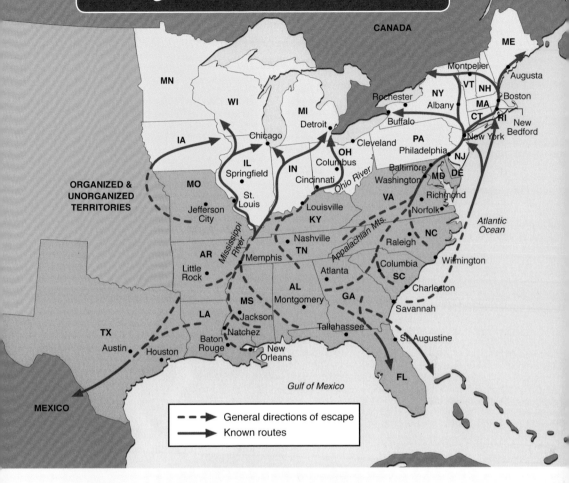

Underground Railroad Circa 1860

Legend:
- `- - - ▶` General directions of escape
- `——▶` Known routes

When the bill was introduced in Congress, furious debate followed. Southerners supported it because it allowed them the opportunity to expand slavery. So-called "free soil" supporters angrily opposed it. Representative Joshua Giddings and Senator Salmon P. Chase, both from Ohio, wrote an appeal to the People of the United States which stated, "We arraign [declare] this bill as a gross violation of a sacred pledge; as a criminal betrayal of precious rights; as part and parcel of an atrocious plot to . . . convert it [a vast region of the country] into a dreary region of despotism, inhabited by masters and slaves."[36] The debate went on for months, with the South pushing for the change and the North resisting. When the issue came up in the House of Representatives, Ohio free-soiler Lewis D. Campbell led a filibuster (a long speech to prevent adoption of a measure generally favored by a majority), which so en-raged House members that they became violent. Both sides exchanged insults and charges. They pulled weapons and threatened to use them. Virginian Henry A. Edmundson had to be restrained from attacking Campbell and was finally arrested. The House had to adjourn to stop the scuffle. In the end, however, there were enough votes to pass the bill, and President Franklin Pierce signed it into law on May 30, 1854.

Harriet Tubman, photographed in 1850, escaped slavery and then became a conductor on the Underground Railroad. Despite poor health, she helped many slaves flee the bonds of slavery.

Bleeding Kansas

Much of the North felt that the Kansas-Nebraska Act was a step in the wrong direction for America. Instead of slavery fading away as they had hoped, it seemed to be expanding. Abraham Lincoln, who was running for Congress in 1854, stated, "We began by declaring that all men are created equal, but now from that beginning we have run down to the other declaration, that for some men to enslave others is 'a sacred right of self-government.'"[37] A group of antislavery activists, free-soil adherents, and others came together that same year to form the Republican Party, its goal being to fight the expansion of slavery.

Meanwhile, settlement in the territories went on. Few slaves were taken into Nebraska, so slavery was not a serious issue there, but Kansas was farther south and bordered Missouri, a slave state. Therefore it was not surprising when 5,000 proslavery Missourians, known as Border Ruffians, were the first to cross into Kansas territory and set up a government that endorsed slavery. At the same time, thousands of free-soil settlers from the North rushed into the territory, too, funded by antislavery organizations such as the New England Emigrant Aid Company. They set up their own government and insisted that their opponents' government had been illegally formed.

It did not take long for the two sides to physically clash. On November 21, 1855, in the so-called "Wakarusa War," free-soiler Charles Dow was shot by a proslavery settler in the Wakarusa River Valley. As a result, the town of Lawrence, a free-soil settlement, was surrounded and attacked by proslavery men. The incident marked the first skirmish in the area that would grow bloodier and become known as "Bleeding Kansas."

The Pottawatomie Massacre

At least 56 people died in "Bleeding Kansas" between 1855 and 1859, and the most renowned killings involved a notorious man named John Brown. Brown was controversial even among abolitionists. He was an incompetent businessman who failed to repay his debts and a devout Christian who did not hesitate to murder. A father of 20 children, he beat them for minor mistakes while at the same time he condemned the cruelty of slavery. And he was hot-tempered, impatient with abolitionists who were not willing to take drastic steps to wipe out slavery. "These men are all talk. What we need is action—action!"[38] he cried.

Brown's favorite Biblical passage was Hebrews 9:22—"Without shedding of blood there is no remission (of sin)"[39]—and he showed that he took the message literally on the night of May 24, 1856. In what became known as the Pottawatomie Massacre, he and a group of men that included four of his sons kidnapped seven proslavery men from their homes near Pottawatomie Creek, led them into the darkness, and then hacked them to death with broadswords.

Brown was involved in another bloody incident on August 30, 1856, at the Battle of Osawatomie. At that time a group of about 300 Missourians led by John W. Reid and Marvin White attacked the free-soil settlement of Osawatomie. With 40 or so supporters, Brown tried to defend the town against the proslavery attackers. There were heavy casualities—Brown claimed to have killed and wounded from 70 to 80 men—but Brown and his men were finally forced to withdraw, leaving the town to be looted and burned.

No Going Back

In what would be his final effort, John Brown led a raid on the federal armory at Harpers Ferry, Virginia (modern-day West Virginia), on October 16, 1859. During the raid, Brown seized the armory, intending to take guns that were stored there and to arm slaves so they would stage an uprising in the South. The attack failed, Brown was captured by federal troops, and his men fled or were captured and killed.

In all, seven people were killed, and ten or more were injured. Brown was tried, found guilty, and sentenced to hang. On December 2, 1859, the morning of his death, he wrote, "I, John Brown, am now quite certain that the crimes of this guilty land will never be purged away but with blood."[40]

The words and actions of John Brown and other abolitionists panicked Southerners who feared that the raid was just the first of many Northern plots to cause a slave rebellion. The Republican Party's choice of Abraham Lincoln as its candidate for president in 1860, however, made secession seem an imminent necessity if they were to save slavery.

The Beating of Charles Sumner

The beating of Charles Sumner on May 22, 1856, demonstrated how deep the hostilities had grown between pro- and antislavery Americans. On the morning of May 19, on the floor of the Senate, Sumner delivered a speech he called "The Crime Against Kansas." In it he accused one of his opponents, South Carolina senator Andrew Butler, of having a mistress—slavery—who was ugly to others but lovely to him.

Butler was not present at the time, but his nephew Congressman Preston Brooks was. Determined to avenge his uncle's name, Brooks entered the Senate chamber two days later and beat Sumner with his cane until the cane broke and Sumner collapsed. The Massachusetts senator was so badly injured that he could not serve again for over three years.

While he recuperated, the *New York Tribune* printed Sumner's speech, and the senator became an antislavery hero. At the same time, Southern newspapers loudly applauded Brooks in print. The *Richmond (VA) Whig* wrote: "A glorious deed! A most glorious deed! Mr. Brooks, of South Carolina, administered to Senator Sumner, a notorious abolitionist from Massachusetts, an effectual and classic caning. We are rejoiced. The only regret we feel is that Mr. Brooks did not employ a slave whip instead of a stick."

American Social History Project, "Southern Newspapers Praise Attack on Charles Sumner," 2011. http://herb.ashp.cuny.edu.

As a *Charleston Mercury* editorial stated on November 3, 1860, "The issue before the country is the extinction of slavery. No man of common sense, who has observed the progress of events, and is not prepared to surrender the institution can doubt that the time for action has come—now or never."[41]

Chapter 3

Slavery Leads to War

When Abraham Lincoln was chosen by the Republican Party to run for president, the North considered him a moderate on slavery. He believed that slavery was wrong and had pledged to stop its spread. But he also stated in 1858 and many times after that, "I believe there is no right, and ought to be no inclination in the people of the free States to enter into the slave States, and interfere with the question of slavery at all."[42]

Southerners did not believe him, however. They called him a "Black Republican" because of his support for black freedom. They viewed his possible election as disastrous, convinced that he did not have the South's welfare at heart. And, because many held Thomas Jefferson's conviction that states did not owe unlimited allegiance to the federal government, they vowed they would leave the Union rather than give up their slaves. One group of South Carolinians proclaimed in the *Charleston Mercury* newspaper on November 15, 1860: "We, the undersigned, citizens of the State of South Carolina, cognizant [aware] of the grave issues which will be inaugurated by the election of a Black Republican President of these United States do hereby form ourselves into an Association . . . for the purpose of sustaining our equality in the Union; or, failing in that, to establish the independence of our State out of it."[43]

The War Begins

Lincoln won the presidential election on November 6, 1860. He got less than 40 percent of the popular vote but more than any other candidate.

His name was not even on the ballot in most Southern states. Before he took office, seven states seceded from the Union and formed the Confederate States of America.

Lincoln did not believe that war was inevitable, but he was determined to hold the Union together no matter the cost. He pointed out that as the nation's leader, he was bound to "hold, occupy, and possess the property and places belonging to the Government,"[44] whether they were in the North or the South. Therefore, he pointed out that the choice to go to war was in the hands of Southerners, and he asked them to think calmly and carefully about their decisions. "In *your* hands, my dissatisfied fellow-countrymen, and not in *mine*, is the momentous issue of civil war. The Government will not assail *you*. You can have no conflict without being yourselves the aggressors. . . . We are not enemies, but friends. We must not be enemies. Though passion may have strained it must not break our bonds of affection."[45]

Despite Lincoln's pleas, on April 12, 1861, Confederate forces attacked federal soldiers stationed at Fort Sumter, South Carolina. Lincoln responded by calling for a volunteer army from each state to recapture federal property. "I appeal to all loyal citizens to favor, facilitate and aid this effort to maintain the honor, the integrity, and the existence of our National Union, and the perpetuity [continuation] of popular government; and to redress [compensate for] wrongs already long enough endured."[46] By May 20, 1861, four more slave states had seceded and joined the Confederacy. The Civil War had officially begun.

"Liberty Must Take the Day"

As both sides called for volunteers and raised armies, it sounded like the nation was going to war over a difference of opinion regarding the importance of states' versus federal rights. Southerners spoke continually of the fact that states had the right to leave the Union if they wished. Union supporters said just the opposite. They claimed that turning against the federal government was an act of treason, a violation of allegiance to one's country. These principles seemed to be so important that everyone was willing to die to uphold them.

The principles were important, but in fact, the reason for war was slavery, and everyone knew it. Without the division that slavery caused, there would have been no need to discuss states' rights versus federal ones. Some Southerners did not want to admit this because slavery was controversial, but slaves realized it from the beginning.

They also realized that their future was at stake. If the North lost, their hopes for freedom would die. If the South could be defeated, slavery would be defeated as well. One slave explained, "Our Union friends Says the(y) are not fighting to free the Negros we are fighting for the union . . . very well let the white fight for what the(y) want and we Negros fight for what we want . . . liberty must take the day."[47]

"Contraband of War"

The upheaval caused by the war made it easier for both slaves and abolitionists to do things that they had not dared to do before. For instance, with most Southern men leaving for battle, slaves were not closely supervised. Many took advantage of the fact and escaped. Those who did so often looked for protection behind Union army lines, which were often just a few miles away. Thousands of escaped slaves joined Union encampments, where commanders like General Benjamin Butler and General John C. Fremont allowed them to remain.

Butler was in charge of Fort Monroe in Virginia, and in May 1861, when the first runaway slaves arrived to seek protection, he put them to work at the fort. When his action was challenged by the slaves' owner, Butler defied the Fugitive Slave Act and refused to return them. Instead he pointed out that Virginia had seceded and was no longer part of the Union. He compared it to a foreign nation and claimed that, according to the law, the federal government did not have to return slaves to foreign nations. "I shall hold these Negroes as contraband of war," he announced. "If [their owner] will come into the fort and take the oath of allegiance to the United States, he shall have his Negroes."[48]

Butler's phrase "contraband of war"—war materiel which by law could be seized by a government—caught the attention of the North. Northerners applauded Butler's way of getting around the law and began using it themselves. In August the US Congress passed the Confiscation Act of 1861, which declared that any property used by the Confederate military, including slaves, could be seized by Union forces. On September 25, 1861, Secretary of the Navy Gideon Welles also issued a directive which paid contrabands who worked for the Union Navy $10 a month plus one ration of food a day. Three weeks later, the Union army did the same, paying male contrabands $8 a month and females $4.

"A Musket on His Shoulder"

As more blacks worked behind the lines, they pushed for the right to enlist and fight in the army as soldiers. Lincoln opposed their efforts, afraid that the move would cause the border slave states to secede. Abolitionists were outraged at his decision, and Frederick Douglass was the most outspoken.

Douglass was a strong believer that blacks should not wait for whites to fight their battles. He had been a slave until he was 20 years old. At that time, he had escaped from the slave state of Maryland to freedom in Massachusetts. After that, he had spent his days speaking and writing about the evils of slavery and the right of blacks to be free. As soon as war broke out he began insisting that the North should use all the men it could get—white and black—in order to win. "Why does the government reject the Negro? Is he not a man? Can he not wield a sword, fire a gun, march and countermarch and obey orders like any other? . . . This is no time to fight only with your white hand and allow your black hand to remain tied."[49]

Other young free blacks agreed with Douglass. Beginning in 1861, black volunteers from Massachusetts and Connecticut formed four regiments in the hope of serving in the Union army. They were not allowed to fight for some time, but the gesture showed that they loved their country and were willing to die for it. Douglass wrote, "Once let the black man get upon his person the brass letter, U.S., let him get an eagle on his button, and a musket on his shoulder and bullets in his pocket, there is no power on earth which can deny that he has earned the right to citizenship."[50]

Lincoln's Decision

By late 1861, Lincoln recognized that if the North was going to win the war and the United States become whole again, the nation could no longer be half slave and half free. No matter what he had promised the South, no matter what the move did to the economy, slavery had to be abolished. Other Northern statesmen were moving in the same direction in their thoughts, and they were acting. In March 1862 Congress passed a law forbidding the army to return slaves to their masters. In April of that same year, it abolished slavery in the District of Columbia. In June it prohibited slavery in all existing federal territories and any that would be formed or acquired in the future.

Lincoln understood that emancipating the slaves would be a huge disruption to the South. So he suggested a plan that had been a favorite of his for decades—paying Southerners in return for giving up their slaves. He stated, "For two hundred years the whole country has . . . regarded and treated the slaves as property. Now, does the mere fact that the North has come suddenly to a contrary opinion give us the right to take the slaves from their owners without compensation?"[51]

By July 1862, however, no slave state that had remained in the Union—the border states of Kentucky, Missouri, Maryland, and Delaware—had taken advantage of compensated emancipation. Left with no other good options, Lincoln decided that he needed to act. An emancipation declaration would unite and inspire the North to support a war that was proving longer and more difficult to win than anyone had imagined. Morally, Lincoln believed, it was also the right thing to do. He determined to make the announcement as soon as the North won a decisive battle, so the declaration would be seen as coming from a position of strength, not desperation.

The Emancipation Proclamation

The victory that Lincoln was waiting for came in September 1862, when Union general George McClellan forced Confederate general Robert E. Lee's army out of Maryland in the Battle of Antietam.

"Forever Free"

In the middle of the Civil War, Abraham Lincoln issued the Emancipation Proclamation on January 1, 1863. The proclamation freed slaves held only in Confederate states but is viewed in history as the document that abolished slavery in America.

Whereas, on the twenty-second day of September, in the year of our Lord one thousand eight hundred and sixty-two, a proclamation was issued by the President of the United States, containing, among other things, the following, to wit:

That on the first day of January, in the year of our Lord one thousand eight hundred and sixty-three, all persons held as slaves within any State or designated part of a State, the people whereof shall then be in rebellion against the United States, shall be then, thenceforward, and forever free; and the Executive Government of the United States, including the military and naval authority thereof, will recognize and maintain the freedom of such persons, and will do no act or acts to repress such persons, or any of them, in any efforts they may make for their actual freedom. . . .

And upon this act, sincerely believed to be an act of justice, warranted by the Constitution, upon military necessity, I invoke the considerate judgment of mankind, and the gracious favor of Almighty God.

National Archives and Records Administration, "The Emancipation Proclamation," January 1, 1863. www.archives.gov.

Although many blacks rejoiced at the news of the Emancipation Proclamation, it promised freedom for Southern slaves only if the North won the Civil War. Rather than wait for that outcome, thousands of slaves made their way to Union lines (as depicted in this hand-colored woodcut).

Immediately thereafter, Lincoln announced that he would issue a formal Emancipation Proclamation on January 1, 1863. At that time, all slaves in states that had seceded from the Union would be granted their freedom. Lincoln was criticized because the proclamation promised freedom for slaves in the Confederacy but did not free slaves in border states. Nevertheless, most ordinary Americans saw it as an official war goal and realized that an enormous first step toward ending a national injustice had been taken. Even Douglass, who wanted nationwide abolition, approved the move. He stated, "I saw in its spirit a life and power far beyond its letter. Its meaning to me was the entire abolition of slavery, wherever the evil could be reached by the Federal arm, and I saw its moral power would extend much further."[52]

Not surprisingly, Southerners loudly condemned the move, fearing that freed slaves might turn on their masters and slaughter them. Confederate president Jefferson Davis told the Southern Congress that the document was "the most execrable measure in the history of guilty man."[53]

On the other hand, Europeans, who had already abolished slavery in their countries, approved the announcement. Henry Adams, aide to the US ambassador to the United Kingdom, commented: "The Emancipation Proclamation has done more for us here than all our former victories and all our diplomacy. It is creating an almost convulsive reaction in our favor all over this country."[54] The Confederacy had long hoped to gain the support of Britain and France, which were dependant on cotton, but the announcement of emancipation tipped the balance in favor of the North and influenced Europeans to stay out of the war.

Black Reaction

For blacks, the Emancipation Proclamation was an event that generations had been dreaming of. Douglass described the mood of thousands of free blacks in Boston on January 1st: "Joy and gladness exhausted all forms of expression, from shouts of praise to sobs and tears. . . . It was one of the most affecting and thrilling occasions I ever witnessed, and a worthy celebration of the first step on the part of the nation in its departure from the thralldom [bondage] of ages."[55]

For slaves in the South, the proclamation was only a promise of freedom if the North won the war. It applied directly to them, but they were still under the control of their Southern masters. Thus, they could run away to the North, wait until Union soldiers arrived to free them sometime during the war, or wait until the war ended. Almost 200,000 blacks left the South when they heard the announcement of freedom. Just as many stayed where they were.

Future author, orator, and political leader Booker T. Washington, who was a child during the war, was one such slave. His emancipation day arrived when the war ended in 1865, and he remembered it clearly:

As the great day drew nearer, there was more singing in the slave quarters than usual. It was bolder, had more ring, and lasted late into the night. Most of the verses of the plantation songs had some reference to freedom. Some man who seemed to be a stranger (a United States officer, I presume) made a little speech and then read a rather long paper—the Emancipation Proclamation, I think. After the reading we were told that we were all free, and could go when and where we pleased. My mother, who was standing by my side, leaned over and kissed her children, while tears of joy ran down her cheeks. She explained to us what it all meant, that this was the day for which she had been so long praying, but fearing that she would never live to see.[56]

"Negroes Will Fight"

After the Emancipation Proclamation took effect, blacks were actively recruited for the Union military. Volunteers from South Carolina, Tennessee, and Massachusetts filled the first authorized black regiments, known as the United States Colored Troops (USCT).

Approximately 175 regiments composed of more than 178,000 free blacks and former slaves served during the last two years of the war. They distinguished themselves in fighting at Port Hudson, Louisiana, in May 1863, in Honey Springs, Indian Territory (now Oklahoma) in July 1863, and at Fort Wagner, South Carolina, also in July 1863. General James Blunt wrote after the battle at Honey Springs, "I never saw such fighting as was done by the Negro regiment. . . . The question that negroes will fight is settled; besides they make better solders in every respect than any troops I have ever had under my command."[57] By war's end, members of the USCT made up nearly one-tenth of all Union troops.

With more men to fight for the North, and the discovery of generals who were willing to fight hard and win battles, the Union began to show its superiority in the war. Ulysses S. Grant was given command of the Union's eastern army in 1864 and organized the armies of William

The men of Company E of the 4th US Colored Troops stand outside their barracks at Fort Lincoln in Washington, DC. More than 178,000 free blacks and former slaves served with the Union army during the last two years of the Civil War.

Tecumseh Sherman, Philip Sheridan, and others to attack the Confederacy from all directions. Grant himself led the Overland Campaign, which ended successfully on April 1, 1865, when the Confederates' attempt to defend Petersburg, Virginia, failed.

The War Ends

Lee finally surrendered to Grant at Appomattox Court House, South Carolina, on April 9, 1865, bringing the war to an end. One New York woman, Caroline Cowles Richards, remembered the North's feelings that day: "Lee has surrendered! and all the people seem crazy in consequence. The bells are ringing, boys and girls, men and women are running through the streets wild with excitement; the flags are all flying, one from the top of our church, and such a 'hurrah boys' generally, I never dreamed of."[58]

"So Full of Hope and Glory"

Early in 1863 the governor of Massachusetts issued the Civil War's first call for black soldiers. Two weeks later more than 1,000 men had volunteered, and by May they were setting off for battle, as the article "The 54th Massachusetts Infantry" describes:

> At nine o'clock on the morning on May 28, 1863, the 54th's 1,007 black soldiers and 37 white officers gathered in the Boston Common and prepared to head to the battlefields of the South. They did so in spite of an announcement by the Confederate Congress that every captured black soldier would be sold into slavery and every white officer in command of black troops would be executed. Cheering well-wishers, including the anti-slavery advocates William Lloyd Garrison, Wendell Phillips and Frederick Douglass, lined Boston's streets. "I know not," Governor Andrew said at the close of the parade, "where in all human history to any given thousand men in arms there has been committed a work at once so proud, so precious, so full of hope and glory as the work committed to you." That evening, the 54th Infantry boarded a transport ship bound for Charleston.

Quoted in History.com, "The 54th Massachusetts Infantry," 2011. www.history.com.

Whites in the South did not feel such jubilation. Their once prosperous economy was in ruins. Cities were destroyed. Farms were unworked. Horses, mules, and cattle were in short supply. Transportation was difficult, as railroads had been wrecked and ruined. There was no money to make improvements, and there was no work force—former slaves—to do the work for free. As Southern matron Mary Chesnut mourned, "Indeed, nothing is left to us now but the bare land, and the debts contracted for the support of hundreds of negroes during the war."[59]

How the former slaves reacted to the war's end depended on their personalities and situations. Some faced the future with anticipation. Some who had been relatively happy with their prewar life remained where they were, working for former masters. Some found themselves in the frightening position of being without a home and without a plan for the future. Freed slave Fountain Hughes remembers, "Now, uh, after we got freed and they turned us out like cattle . . . we didn't have nowhere to go. And we didn't have nobody to boss us, and, uh, we didn't know nothing. . . . I know, I remember one night, I was out after I, I was free, and I didn't have nowhere to go. I didn't have nowhere to sleep. I didn't know what to do."[60]

The Thirteenth Amendment

The end of slavery marked the beginning of a new era in American history. Lincoln and others were concerned, however, that the Emancipation Proclamation would be seen as an incomplete or even temporary measure that could be modified or revoked in the future. They wanted to make black freedom the permanent law of the land, and they believed the best way to do that was by an amendment to the Constitution.

Amending the US Constitution was a serious and uncommon occurrence. The 12 amendments that existed up to 1865 had all been adopted within 15 years of forming the Constitution. The first 10—the Bill of Rights—were ratified in 1791, the 11th in 1795, and the 12th in 1804. Nevertheless, on January 11, 1864—before the war ended—Senator John B. Henderson of Missouri submitted a proposal for a constitutional amendment abolishing slavery. On February 8 of that year, Republican senator Charles Sumner of Massachusetts also submitted a proposal for an amendment that would abolish slavery and guarantee racial equality. Other proposals were also submitted at the same time.

The Senate took until April 8, 1864 to reconcile the differences in the bills and write and pass the proposed amendment. In the end, it simply stated "Neither slavery nor involuntary servitude, except as a punishment for crime whereof the party shall have been duly convicted, shall exist within the United States, or any place subject to their jurisdiction."[61] The proposal was then sent on to the House of Representatives which passed it on January 31, 1865. The legislatures of 27 of the then 36 states ratified it by December 6, 1865, and Secretary of State William Henry Seward proclaimed it to be law on December 16 of that year.

Even though slavery had been officially abolished, however, division over black civil and political rights remained. Blacks wanted equality, beginning with the right to vote. Douglass stated specifically, "Slavery is not abolished until the black man has the ballot."[62] White Southerners, on the other hand, had different ideas. The abolition of slavery had been forced upon them, but they had no intention of treating blacks as equals. It was not long before they were passing new discriminatory laws so they could be sure that old patterns of white superiority would continue in the coming decades.

Chapter 4

Free but Unequal

The South was defeated, slavery was abolished, and the Union was restored. The conflicting views that had caused the war had not changed, however. In fact, the bitterness of defeat only made Southerners less willing to accept former slaves as equals. Therefore, the first struggle over the rights and the status of ex-slaves began immediately after the war and lasted until 1877.

That struggle took place during the period known as Reconstruction, when the South was being reorganized and reintegrated back into the Union. During that time, black political, economic, and social rights advanced or regressed depending on whether radical or conservative politicians were in power. Historian Steven Mintz writes, "Reconstruction, one of the most turbulent and controversial eras in American history . . . witnessed America's first experiment in interracial democracy. Just as the fate of slavery was central to the meaning of the Civil War, so the divisive politics of Reconstruction turned on the status the former slaves would assume in the reunited nation."[63]

Lincoln's Reconstruction

Planning for Reconstruction actually began during the war, when Abraham Lincoln and Congress considered what would need to be done to bring the South back into the Union when the war was over. Lincoln held moderate views on Reconstruction. He had no interest in punishing the South for its rebellion. Rather, he wanted to reunite the country as quickly and painlessly as possible. He stated, "With malice toward none; with charity for all; with firmness in the right, as God gives us to see the right, let us strive on to finish the work we are in; to bind up the nation's wounds; to care for him who shall have borne the battle, and for his widow and his orphan . . . to do all which may achieve and cherish a just and lasting peace among ourselves and with all nations."[64]

Lincoln had initially suggested a Ten Percent Plan of Reconstruction. Under this plan a state was eligible to reenter the Union after 10 percent of its white male population took an oath of loyalty and supported emancipation of slaves. By such moderation, Lincoln hoped to minimize the bitterness of defeat and encourage Southerners to cooperate in setting up and carrying out new antislavery policies.

Lincoln's plan did not spell out new rights for blacks, but he was aware that they would face significant challenges in their new lives. They were uneducated, powerless, and poor. They had never had to find jobs before. They had no homes except those belonging to former masters. To aid them in all these areas, therefore, on March 3, 1865, Lincoln signed the Freedmen's Bureau Bill into law. It created the Bureau of Refugees, Freedmen, and Abandoned Lands (shortened to Freedmen's Bureau), a federal agency designed to provide food, clothing, fuel, and advice to Southern blacks. It oversaw new relations between freedmen and their former masters. The bureau was to expire one year after the termination of the war, but in fact it was in operation until 1871.

Johnson's Reconstruction Plan

Lincoln was assassinated by actor John Wilkes Booth on April 14, 1865, five days after the war ended. The vice president, Andrew Johnson, succeeded Lincoln as president and proved to be as moderate in his Reconstruction policies as his predecessor. His moderation was based in part on the fact that he had been a US senator from Tennessee, a Confederate state, when the war broke out. He had not sided with the Confederacy, and he had supported emancipation, but he still had sympathy for the Southern point of view. He wrote in 1866, "This is a country for white men, and by God, as long as I am President, it shall be a government for white men."[65]

A little over a month after the war's end, on May 29, 1865, Johnson granted anmesty and pardon to most Southerners who had taken part in the rebellion. No pardons were granted to large landowners. No pardons were granted to civil and diplomatic officials, officers above the rank of colonel, anyone who left the US military to fight for the Confederacy, anyone educated in the US military academies, and/or anyone who left home in the North to go south.

Those who were excluded from the pardon, however, had only to individually plead their case to the president, and they could receive amnesty. Then, if they took a loyalty oath promising they would support the Constitution and abide by US laws, their property rights were restored. After enough residents of a state took the loyalty oath, the process of reestablishing state governments and adopting new state constitutions began.

Though finally freed of the bonds of slavery, blacks in Southern towns like this one struggled to reconstruct their lives shortly after the Civil War. They were poor and uneducated; they had no homes of their own and no experience looking for work.

Black Codes

By December 1865 all of the former Confederate states except Texas had applied for readmission to the Union. At that time Johnson declared that the goals of unity and emancipation had been achieved and Reconstruction was complete. With no conditions to hinder them, white Southerners almost immediately began to take control of their state legislatures again. Former politicians were reelected to Congress, and governments began passing laws known as Black Codes that reflected the determination of white Southerners to keep blacks subordinate.

Black Codes limited blacks' civil liberties, regulated their labor, and kept them economically and socially disadvantaged. Laws varied from state to state but could apply to everything from personal affairs to legal issues. For example, Texas made it a crime for black laborers to use offensive language in the presence of their employers or their employers' families. Other states required that blacks sign annual contracts that tied them to a job for a year at a time. They denied blacks the right to testify against whites in court or to serve on juries. They blocked blacks from getting good jobs, denied them the right to rent or purchase land, and forbade them to gather in certain places at certain times of the day. Segregation was codified as well. For instance, blacks could not ride on white streetcars or attend white schools. "No negro or mulatto [person of mixed Caucasian and Negro ancestry] shall be admitted to attend any public school in this state, except such schools as may be established exclusively for colored persons,"[66] stated a law passed in Arkansas in 1867.

Those blacks who did not obey Black Codes were punished by beatings, imprisonment, or hanging. Government representative Carl Schurz wrote in late 1865, "During my two days sojourn at Atlanta, one Negro was stabbed with fatal effect on the street, and three were poisoned, one of whom died. While I was at Montgomery, one Negro was cut across the throat evidently with intent to kill, and another was shot."[67]

Radical Republicans

Black Codes outraged former abolitionists. It was apparent that Southerners were blatantly creating laws that were almost as oppressive and controlling as slavery had been. *New York Tribune* editor Horace Greeley wrote, "[The first fruits of Reconstruction promise] a most deplorable harvest, and the sooner we gather the tares [weeds], plow the ground again and sow new seed the better."[68]

Some of the most outraged were members of Congress known as the Radical Republicans. They were men led by Representative Thaddeus Stevens and Senator Charles Sumner, and were seen as radical because they believed that Reconstruction needed to punish former Southern leaders while giving the greatest possible help to newly freed slaves. Sumner stated in 1864:

> It is evident, then, that the freedmen are not idlers. They desire work. But in their helpless condition they have not the ability to obtain it without assistance. They are alone, friendless, and uninformed. The curse of slavery is still upon them. Somebody must take them by the hand; not to support them but simply to help them to that work which will support them. . . . Without such intervention, many of those poor people, freed by our acts in the exercise of a military necessity, will be left to perish.[69]

Radical Republicans also believed that it was Congress's job, not the president's, to set the Reconstruction requirements that the South needed to meet before they could reenter the Union. Stevens wrote, "Congress is the sovereign power, because the people speak through them; and Andrew Johnson must learn that he is your servant, and that as Congress shall order, he must obey."[70] Not all Republicans were radical, but even moderate members of Congress were concerned that ex-Confederate leaders would regain control of the South and reignite the rebellion and the war. Thus they went along with the Radicals and formed a majority that was able to vote for and effectively gain significant political, social, and civil rights for former slaves.

Congress's Reconstruction plan was based on a bill proposed by Senator Benjamin F. Wade and Representative Henry Winter Davis in February 1864. The Wade-Davis Bill required that 50 percent of a state's white males take an "ironclad oath" before the state would be readmitted to the

Congress and Reconstruction

Representative Thaddeus Stevens of Pennsylvania was one of the most vocal members of the Radical Republicans during the time President Johnson and Congress wrestled for power. In a speech given on December 18, 1865, Stevens hammers home the point that Congress must be in charge of Reconstruction and that freed slaves must be helped if they are to adjust to their new lives.

Congress must create States and declare when they are entitled to be represented. Then each House must judge whether the members presenting themselves from a recognized State possess the requisite qualifications of age, residence, and citizenship; and whether the election and returns are according to law.

But this is not all that we ought to do before inveterate [confirmed] rebels are invited to participate in our legislation. We have turned, or are about to turn, loose four million slaves without a hut to shelter them or a cent in their pockets. The infernal laws of slavery have prevented them from acquiring an education, understanding the common laws of contract, or of managing the ordinary business of life. This Congress is bound to provide for them until they can take care of themselves. If we do not furnish them with homesteads, and hedge them around with protective laws; if we leave them to the legislation of their late masters, we had better have left them in bondage.

From Revolution to Reconstruction, "Thaddeus Stevens, Speech of December 18, 1865," University of Groningen, Netherlands, 2010. www.let.rug.nl.

Union. "Ironclad" meant that it was rigid and unbreakable and allowed for no exceptions or variations. In taking it, individuals had to swear that they had never supported the Confederacy or been one of its soldiers. Because most of the South's statesmen had done one or the other or both, this effectively disqualified them from taking the oath.

Congress realized that such a restriction was going to slow the South's reentry into the Union. It would take time to get states reorganized since most of their former leaders were barred from participating in government. That was acceptable, however, because Congress wanted a radically different South than before the war. They wanted to use a combination of legislation and close oversight to ensure that blacks had opportunities equal to those of whites and to force whites to accept blacks as equals.

Therefore Congress passed four Reconstruction Acts in 1867 and 1868, the first of which declared martial law in the South and divided the region into five military districts. These districts were governed by Union generals and policed by the US military, which was still present in the South. In addition, Congress required that each state draft a new state constitution, which needed to be approved by Congress. The states also were required to ratify the Fourteenth Amendment and to grant voting rights to black men.

Citizenship and the Right to Vote

The Reconstruction Acts were not the only laws Congress passed after the war. The Civil Rights Act, passed in 1866, stated that anyone born in the United States was a citizen. The act also affirmed the right of freedmen to make and sign contracts, to sue, and to buy, lease, and transfer personal property.

Congress also passed two constitutional amendments in 1866 and 1869. These, combined with the Thirteenth Amendment, became known as Reconstruction Amendments. The Fourteenth Amendment was ratified in 1868 and provided for black citizenship, stating that all persons born or naturalized in the United States were citizens. It prohibited state and local governments from depriving persons of life, liberty, or property without certain steps being taken to ensure fairness. It also required each state to provide equal protection under the law to all people within its boundaries.

The Fifteenth Amendment, passed in early February 1870, gave blacks the right to vote. It stated that the government could not deprive a citizen of that right because of "race, color, or previous condition of servitude [slavery]."[71] Douglass rejoiced, "At last the black man has a future. The black man is free, the black man is a citizen, the black man is enfranchised. . . . Never was revolution more complete."[72]

New Opportunities

It was not long before blacks began to take advantage of the new opportunities and rights afforded them. About 700,000 registered to vote in the South, and when it came time for state constitutional conventions to be held, black leaders participated in all of them. The state constitutions they helped craft expanded women's rights, provided debt relief, and established more state-funded schools.

Blacks of all ages were quick to take advantage of the latter. They had been forbidden even to learn to read before the war, and they knew that literacy was one of the paths to self-determination. Their schools were segregated, so no whites attended, but most blacks approved of the setup because they wanted a safe environment for their children and realized that black schools provided jobs for black teachers.

Black leaders also ran for office for the first time. Hiram Rhodes Revels of Mississippi became the first black elected to the US Senate, and John Willis Menard of Louisiana became the first black elected to the US House of Representatives. One of Revel's contemporaries, John Roy Lynch, remarked of Revels: "He made a profound impression upon all who heard him. It impressed those who heard [him] that Revels was not only a man of great natural ability but that he was also a man of superior attainments."[73]

Struggle for Power

Advances made by blacks did not sit well with Southerners, especially with Johnson. Because his Reconstruction plan differed widely from those of the Radicals, by 1866 full-scale political warfare existed between the president and Congress. Johnson vetoed 21 bills passed by Congress during his term, and the Radicals overrode 15 of his vetoes.

The struggle reached a crisis in late 1867. On March 3 of that year, Congress passed the Tenure of Office Act over Johnson's veto. The act denied the president the right to remove any executive officer who had been appointed by a past president without Congress's approval. It was created specifically to stop Johnson from firing Secretary of War Edwin M. Stanton. Lincoln had appointed Stanton, and the secretary had a great deal of power not only in his own department but also in the State and Treasury Departments. He even used the Secret Service, assigned to protect the president, to spy on Johnson. Johnson felt that the Tenure of Office Act was unconstitutional, and he suspended Stanton on August 5, 1867. Congress reinstated him on January 7, 1868. Johnson fired him on February 21.

Three days later, on February 24, the House of Representatives voted 126 to 47 in favor of a resolution to impeach the president, charging him with high crimes and misdemeanors. Impeachment is the process in which an official is accused of unlawful activity and, if found guilty, is removed from office. The impeachment resolution read in part:

> Andrew Johnson, President of the United States, . . . in violation of the Constitution and laws of the United States, on the 21st day of February, in the year of our Lord 1868, at Washington, in the District of Columbia, did unlawfully conspire . . . to hinder and prevent Edwin M. Stanton, . . . the Secretary for the Department of War, duly appointed under the laws of the United States, from holding said office of Secretary for the Department of War.[74]

Impeachment

A US president had never been impeached before, so the country was not familiar with what was involved. Americans soon learned that it was a two-step process. First, the House of Representatives passed, by a simple majority, the articles of impeachment. Those articles constituted the formal allegation or allegations. With their passage Johnson was indicted, and the second step of his impeachment began: trial before the Senate. Chief Justice of the United States Samuel Chase presided over the proceedings. To convict the accused, a two-thirds majority of the senators present was required, and conviction would automatically remove Johnson from office.

Johnson's impeachment trial began on March 5, 1868, and continued until May 16, when the final vote was taken. It resulted in a verdict of "not guilty"—the final count was one short of the number required for conviction. Republican senator James Grimes, who voted for acquittal, stated, "However widely . . . I may and do differ with the President respecting his political views and measure, and however deeply I have regretted, and do regret the differences between himself and the Congress of the United States, I am not able to record my vote that he is guilty of high crimes and misdemeanors by reason of those differences."[75]

Despite his acquittal, Johnson was so unpopular that he did not receive the Democratic nomination to be their candidate in the 1868 presidential election. Instead they nominated the chairman of the Democratic convention, Horatio Seymour, who was also a strong supporter of moderate Reconstruction policies. General Ulysses S. Grant ran on the Republican ticket. Grant was one of the most popular men in the North due to his success in ending the Civil War. He easily won the election on November 3, 1868.

Southerners Rebel Again

White Southerners endured congressional Reconstruction with deep resentment. They had endured incredible hardships during the war for the sake of secession, and they hated being back in the Union, ruled by their former enemies. They were virtually stripped of their legal rights and privileges. They had to watch free blacks and Northerners restructure their states in ways that seemed to them unfair, illegal, and immoral. Angry, bitter, and frustrated, some decided to strike back. In December

1865 in Pulaski, Tennessee, six veterans of the Confederate Army—
John C. Lester, James R. Crowe, John D. Kennedy, Calvin Jones, Rich-
ard R. Reed, and Frank O. McCord—came together to form the Ku
Klux Klan (KKK), an organization with the goal of intimidating blacks

Vengeful Southerners hid their identities behind robes and hoods or
masks and kidnapped, tortured, and killed freed black slaves. Members
of the Ku Klux Klan, two of whom appear in a photograph taken in
Alabama in 1868, sought to restore white supremacy in the South after
the Civil War.

and black supporters in order to restore white supremacy in the South. Targets could include Republicans, schoolteachers, black ministers, and a host of others.

The idea of retaliation proved popular, and other groups of men quickly formed their own KKK groups throughout the South. To keep their identities secret, avoid arrest, and frighten victims, Klan members dressed in white sheets or robes. They wore hoods and grotesque masks. They staged eerie silent marches down main streets and burned crosses on their targets' properties. They made midnight raids in which they kidnapped victims and beat, whipped, mutilated, or hanged them. Former slave Ben Johnson remembered one event he witnessed shortly after the end of the war:

> I never will forget when they hung Cy Guy. They hung him for a scandalous insult to a white woman an' they comed after him a hundred strong.
>
> They tries him there in the woods, an' they scratches Cy's arm to get some blood, an' with that blood they writes that he shall hang 'tween the heavens and the earth till he is dead, dead, dead, and that any [black] what takes down the body shall be hanged too.
>
> Well sir, the next morning there he hung, right over the road an' the sentence hanging over his head. Nobody would bother with that body for four days an' there it hung, swinging in the wind, but the fourth day the sheriff comes an' takes it down.[76]

Other white supremacy groups, such as the Knights of the White Camellia, the Red Shirts, and the White League, were created as well. Due to their actions, thousands of individuals were killed, injured, driven from their homes, or suffered property damage. In 1871 Congress passed the Ku Klux Klan Act, which allowed the US Army to suppress Klan violence. Hundreds of men were arrested. Some leaders were tried and received prison sentences. By 1872 the reign of terror had abated, but Klan activities never entirely ceased in the South.

The Freedmen's Bureau

Congress created the Bureau of Refugees, Freedmen, and Abandoned Lands in March 1865 to help Southern blacks transition from slavery to freedom. It was run by the War Department, and its first commissioner was General O.O. Howard, a Civil War veteran who was sympathetic to blacks.

The Freedmen's Bureau, as it came to be called, not only helped 4 million Southern blacks, but also poor whites who had lacked power and opportunities before the war. It helped introduce a system of free labor, settled disputes and enforced contracts between white landowners and their black labor force, and secured justice for blacks in state courts.

Education, however, was the most renowned accomplishment of the bureau. It spent nearly $5 million to establish some 3,000 schools throughout the South. As early as 1865, 90,000 former slaves were enrolled as students; the oldest was 105 years old. Attendance rates at the schools were near 80 percent, unlike white schools where attendance rates were about 40 percent.

The Bureau also established a number of colleges and training schools for blacks seeking a higher education. They included Howard University in Washington, DC, (named for General Howard) and Hampton University (formerly Hampton Institute) in Virginia. Hampton's most famous alumnus was Booker T. Washington, who stated "Not even Heaven presented more attractions for me at that time than did the Hampton Normal and Agricultural Institute in Virginia."

Booker T. Washington, *Up from Slavery: An Autobiography*. Garden City, NY: Doubleday, 1901, p. 42, online edition, Documenting the American South, 2004. http://docsouth.unc.edu.

Redemption

Despite the harsh requirements imposed by the government, by the end of 1870 all Southern states had been readmitted to the Union and were represented in Congress. In May 1872 a more moderate Congress passed an Amnesty Act, which gave almost all who had been excluded from holding office the right to participate in government again. Almost immediately after his inauguration in 1877, President Rutherford B. Hayes ordered federal troops removed from Confederate states, bringing Reconstruction to an end.

At the same time, new national problems such as government corruption and an economic depression claimed the attention of the nation. Reconstruction became less of a priority, and "home rule"—the equivalent of white rule—was reestablished. White conservative Southerners began regaining power and "redeeming" their states from radical control by once again passing discriminatory laws.

Gradually, racial injustice, white supremacy, and segregation reappeared in the South. Americans noticed, but they did not care enough to act. To some, advancing civil rights for blacks seemed unnecessary and undesirable. For others, such goals seemed unachievable. The effort had been made, and it had failed. Now they had other things on their minds. As historian Eric Foner writes, "After the end of Reconstruction, it would take nearly a century for the nation to begin to come to terms once again with that era's political and economic agenda, and with the continuing struggle for genuine freedom by the descendants of slavery."[77]

Chapter 5

What Is the Legacy of the Abolition of Slavery?

The abolition of slavery was a momentous event in American history, taking the country one step closer to its professed belief that all men are created equal. After years of debate Americans had taken a stand on an immoral institution and eradicated it. As a result, African Americans and their families could no longer be bought and sold. They had more choices than ever before when it came to living and working. They could get an education and better themselves, and they did. By the beginning of the twentieth century the majority of African Americans could read and write.

Despite such progress, a legacy of racism and discrimination almost cancelled out the good that abolition had produced. In both the North and South, blacks were not granted full equality in society. They had to work harder than whites for everything from getting a college education to getting raises in the workplace. Such conditions were most dire from 1877 to 1965, when Jim Crow Laws and discriminatory policies took away many of the gains made during Reconstruction, essentially legalizing blacks' place in society as second-class citizens.

Separate but Equal

Black rights that had been gained during congressional Reconstruction began to be reversed about 1877. All-white legislatures in the South could not deny anyone the right to vote because of race, but they could create other standards that had to be met before a voter could be registered. For instance, he needed to pay a poll tax, pass a literacy test proving he could read, and/or show that he owned property. Blacks who were poor and uneducated usually could not meet such requirements and thus lost the right to vote.

When blacks contested instances of injustice and discrimination, judicial rulings did not always support civil rights. For instance, in 1883, several blacks sued theaters, hotels, and transit companies for refusing them admittance because of their race. The Supreme Court ruled against them, determining that the Civil Rights Act passed in 1875 was unconstitutional. That act guaranteed that

> all persons within the jurisdiction of the United States shall be entitled to the full and equal enjoyment of the accommodations, advantages, facilities, and privileges of inns, public conveyances on land or water, theaters, and other places of public amusement; subject only to the conditions and limitations established by law, and applicable alike to citizens of every race and color, regardless of any previous condition of servitude.[78]

The court based its decision on the fact that Congress did not have the right to regulate private behavior.

In the 1896 *Plessy v. Ferguson* case the Supreme Court ruled that a Louisiana law that required blacks to use separate railcars from whites did not reduce their privileges nor deprive them of equal protection that the Fourteenth Amendment required. This decision effectively legitimized the segregation of American society under what became known as the separate but equal doctrine. It was applied to other facilities ranging from restaurants to swimming pools, and it allowed whites to segregate blacks by providing separate entrances, seating, or sets of facilities. Almost every public building became segregated, but equality was often ignored. Goods and services offered to blacks were usually of lower quality than those offered to whites. Natchez, Mississippi, resi-

Who Was Jim Crow?

Jim Crow laws were well known in the United States through the 1960s. In the article "From Terror to Triumph," historian Ronald L.F. Davis explains the source of the term and a little of its history.

> The term Jim Crow originated in a song performed by Daddy Rice, a white minstrel show entertainer in the 1830s. Rice covered his face with charcoal to resemble a black man, and then sang and danced a routine in caricature of a silly black person. By the 1850s, this Jim Crow character, one of several stereotypical images of black inferiority in the nation's popular culture, was a standard act in the minstrel shows of the day. How it became a term synonymous with the brutal segregation and disfranchisement of African Americans in the late nineteenth-century is unclear. What is clear, however, is that by 1900, the term was generally identified with those racist laws and actions that deprived African Americans of their civil rights by defining blacks as inferior to whites, as members of a caste of subordinate people.

Ronald L.F. Davis, "From Terror to Triumph: Historical Overview," History of Jim Crow, 2011. www.jimcrowhistory.org.

dent Willie Wallace remembered, "We didn't play baseball together. We didn't play football together. We'd play black schools in Mississippi. White schools played white schools. . . . I had no idea coming up how we were being treated badly [and] the whites were being treated better because I never went to see a white neighborhood to see how badly we were being treated."[79]

Jim Crow Laws

The laws that legalized segregation in the post–Civil War South became known as Jim Crow laws, and Northerners applied many of them to blacks in their communities as well. Jim Crow laws were based on the assumption that whites were superior to blacks and that blacks needed to act as inferiors in any activity involving the two races. In everyday life, this meant that blacks could not sit near whites in restaurants, buses, cars, theaters, or other public places. Blacks could not offer to shake hands with white people. They could not look white people in the eye. They could not live in white neighborhoods or attend white schools.

Especially in the South, any behavior toward white women that might be construed as familiarity on a black man's part was forbidden and could even have deadly consequences. For instance, in Mississippi in August 1955, 14-year-old Emmett Till was kidnapped, beaten, shot, and dumped in the Tallahatchie River for allegedly having whistled at a white woman. The two men who killed Till were arrested for murder but were acquitted by an all-white jury. They were later featured in a magazine article where they boasted about committing the murder. One of them, J.W. Milam, did not hesitate to use the most derogatory terms possible when explaining his actions. "As long as I live and can do anything about it, niggers are gonna stay in their place. Niggers ain't gonna vote where I live. If they did, they'd control the government. They ain't gonna go to school with my kids. And when a nigger gets close to mentioning sex with a white woman, he's tired o' livin'."[80]

Jim Crow laws did not just apply to social situations. Black Americans were rarely able to own the stores or businesses where they worked. Many were limited to menial or blue-collar jobs and worked as custodians, construction workers, field workers, and housekeepers. Most made only enough money to live in dilapidated shacks or poorly maintained public housing. Ronald L.F. Davis writes, "It was a daily battle for one's life, self-respect, and basic civil rights. For most African Americans, this struggle forged a strength of character and an incredible sense of endurance that enabled them not only to survive individually but to prevail culturally as well."[81]

Resisting Jim Crow

Despite a lack of public interest in civil rights in the early 1900s, black and white activists spoke out and took steps to counter the injustice of Jim Crow oppression. Two black leaders of the early twentieth century were Booker T. Washington and W.E.B. Du Bois. Washington, who had been born into slavery, believed that education and cooperation with supportive whites were the best ways to overcome racism. He became friends with white philanthropists such as Standard Oil magnate Henry Huttleston Rogers; Sears, Roebuck and Company president Julius Rosenwald; and George Eastman, inventor and founder of Kodak; who were happy to support his educational efforts.

Du Bois took a more proactive stance. In 1905, with civil rights activist William Monroe Trotter, he founded the Niagara Movement, a group named for the mighty current of change it wanted to effect in North America. The movement helped pave the way for groups such as the National Association for the Advancement of Colored People (NAACP), an interracial organization that was founded in 1909. By the 1920s the NAACP was conducting scores of lawsuits in defense of black civil liberties and civil rights. It also lobbied Congress to pass a federal antilynching bill. Although this effort did not succeed, the exposure and pressure exerted by the NAACP greatly reduced the number of violent incidents against blacks.

In the 1930s the NAACP grew powerful enough to begin challenging discrimination and segregation in the US Supreme Court. One of those cases involved elections. In 1944 in *Smith v. Allwright*, the Supreme Court ruled against the legality of so-called white primaries, in which only white Americans were allowed to determine which top candidates would run for office. This had effectively limited black's choices in elections and discouraged them from voting. Another of the cases brought by the NAACP involved education. In 1954, in the landmark case of *Brown v. the Topeka Board of Education*, the Supreme Court reversed its support of the separate but equal doctrine, effectively declaring that segregated facilities, including schools, were unconstitutional. Decisions like these paved the way for a sea of civil rights litigation and legislation in the 1950s and 1960s.

The Montgomery Bus Boycott

One landmark challenge to Jim Crow laws occurred on December 1, 1955, in Montgomery, Alabama. That day, NAACP member Rosa Parks decided to defy the separate but equal policy of Montgomery's transit system—she refused to give up her seat in a public bus to make room for a white passenger. Under Montgomery's system, white people who boarded the bus took seats in the front rows, filling the bus toward the back, while black people who boarded took seats in the back rows, filling the bus toward the front. If the bus was full, the two

Rosa Parks's refusal to give up her seat to a white bus passenger in December 1955 sparked a months-long bus boycott in Montgomery, Alabama. Parks, being fingerprinted by police in February 1956, and others were arrested during the boycott.

sections met. Then if more blacks boarded the bus, they had to stand. If another white person boarded, however, everyone in the black row nearest the front had to get up, so that a new row for white people could be created.

Parks's civil disobedience resulted in her arrest. She was found guilty and fined $10 plus a court cost of $4. But when local NAACP leader E.D. Nixon learned of her arrest, he called for a one-day citywide bus boycott, during which no black or NAACP supporter would ride a bus. Fliers that were passed out at the time read in part:

> Another woman has been arrested and thrown in jail because she refused to get up out of her seat on the bus for a white person to sit down. This has to be stopped. Negroes have rights too, for if Negroes did not ride the buses, they could not operate. Three-fourths of the riders are Negro, yet we are arrested, or have to stand over empty seats. If we do not do something to stop these arrests, they will continue.[82]

The one-day boycott turned into a 381-day protest. It proved extremely effective. Blacks walked, carpooled, and used other means of transportation, and the city transit system lost 80 percent of its income. Finally, on December 20, 1956, the Supreme Court declared that the Alabama and Montgomery laws requiring segregated buses were unconstitutional. One of Montgomery's most charismatic leaders, Martin Luther King Jr., announced the end of the strike:

> This morning the long awaited mandate from the United States Supreme Court concerning bus segregation came to Montgomery. This mandate expresses in terms that are crystal clear that segregation in public transportation is both legally and sociologically invalid. In the light of this mandate . . . the year old protest against city busses is officially called off, and the Negro citizens of Montgomery are urged to return to the busses tomorrow morning on a non-segregated basis.[83]

Southern Christian Leadership Conference

The Montgomery bus boycott marked the beginning of King's civil rights activism. A Baptist minister, he had decided early on in his career that a policy of nonviolent resistance would help blacks gain greater equality than acts of violence. He believed activism needed to be strong, but it also needed to be just and peaceful. He stated in 1955, "Let us be Christian in all of our actions. But I want to tell you this evening that it is not enough for us to talk about love, love is one of the pivotal points of the Christian faith. There is another side called justice. And justice is really love in calculation. Justice is love correcting that which revolts against love."[84]

After the victory in Montgomery, King and other black American leaders formed an organization to coordinate and support other non-violent boycotts and protests as a method of desegregating the South. In 1957 they formed the Negro Leaders Conference on Nonviolent Integration. The name was soon changed to the Southern Christian Leadership Conference (SCLC). The organization was controversial even in the black community because many black leaders believed that segregation should be challenged in the courts, not on the streets. They feared that direct action would arouse needless white resistance, hostility, and violence. In their eyes, the social-political activity of the SCLC amounted to dangerous radicalism.

Despite the opposition, the nonviolent activism continued. King and the SCLC were driving forces behind protests in Albany, Georgia; Birmingham, Alabama; St. Augustine, Florida; and Selma, Alabama. The campaigns became known as the civil rights movement, and the era came to be called the "Second Reconstruction" because it helped advance the civil rights revolution begun by the post–Civil War Congress and embodied in the Fourteenth and Fifteenth Amendments.

Civil Rights Marches

In addition to protests and boycotts, civil rights participants began to use mass marches to draw attention to issues they believed needed to be addressed. The first of such marches was the 1963 March on Washington for

An Official Apology

On June 18, 2009, the US Senate and House of Representatives issued an apology to African Americans for slavery and racial discrimination that had occurred in the United States in the past. A portion of that document entitled S.Con.Res.26 reads as follows:

> Whereas during the history of the Nation, the United States has grown into a symbol of democracy and freedom around the world;
>
> Whereas the legacy of African-Americans is interwoven with the very fabric of the democracy and freedom of the United States;
>
> Whereas millions of Africans and their descendants were enslaved in the United States and the 13 American colonies from 1619 through 1865; . . .
>
> Whereas it is important for the people of the United States, who legally recognized slavery through the Constitution and the laws of the United States, to make a formal apology for slavery and for its successor, Jim Crow, so they can move forward and seek reconciliation, justice, and harmony for all people of the United States: Now, therefore, be it
>
> Resolved by the Senate (the House of Representatives concurring) . . . the Congress—
>
> (A) acknowledges the fundamental injustice, cruelty, brutality, and inhumanity of slavery and Jim Crow laws;
>
> (B) apologizes to African-Americans on behalf of the people of the United States, for the wrongs committed against them and their ancestors who suffered under slavery and Jim Crow laws; and
>
> (C) expresses its recommitment to the principle that all people are created equal and endowed with inalienable rights to life, liberty, and the pursuit of happiness, and calls on all people of the United States to work toward eliminating racial prejudices, injustices, and discrimination from our society.

Library of Congress, "111th Congress, 1st Session, S. Con. Res. 26 in the House of Representatives," June 18, 2009. http://thomas.loc.gov.

Jobs and Freedom, in which a quarter of a million people marched into Washington, DC, and congregated at the Lincoln Memorial. There they heard King deliver his now-famous "I Have a Dream" speech. Speaking of the fact that blacks were still not free of the racism and discrimination that came with slavery, King expressed his hope that someday all Americans would experience racial justice and equality.

Three more marches in 1965 marked the political and emotional peak of the American civil rights movement. The first march took place on March 7, 1965. It became known as "Bloody Sunday" after 600 people tried to march from Selma to Montgomery to highlight their demand for voting rights. En route they were attacked by state and local police with billy clubs and tear gas and had to turn back.

Despite this type of adversity, many rallied for a second march two days later. This was a symbolic repeat of the first and resulted in 2,500 protesters holding a prayer meeting outside Selma before returning to the city. That night, three white ministers who had joined the march were attacked and beaten with clubs. Unitarian minister James Reeb died of his wounds.

"The Battle Is in Our Hands"

The third march on March 21 included 300 people and lasted for three days as marchers sucessfully walked from Selma to Montgomery. This time they were joined by thousands of sympathizers as they entered the city. Again, Martin Luther King Jr. encouraged his listeners: "The battle is in our hands. And we can answer with creative nonviolence the call to higher ground to which the new directions of our struggle summons us. . . . The road ahead is not altogether a smooth one. . . . There are no broad highways that lead us easily and inevitably to quick solutions. But we must keep going."[85]

Because the participants remained peaceful despite violence used against them, the marches had a positive effect on the nation and on leaders in Washington, DC. In 1964 President Lyndon Baines Johnson signed the Civil Rights Act of 1964. It specifically prohibited discrimination in voting, education, and the use of public facilities.

The pace of change through peaceful activism was too slow for some young black Americans, who turned to the Black Power movement. Members of that movement raise their fists in the Black Power salute in 1969 in San Francisco, California.

This time, the Supreme Court upheld the law's application to the private sector.

In 1965 Johnson presented another bill to Congress that would later pass and become the Voting Rights Act of 1966. The act established extensive federal oversight of elections in states that had a history of discriminatory voting practices. Johnson stated, "[Civil rights] must be our cause, too, because it is not just Negroes but really it is all of us who must overcome the crippling legacy of bigotry and injustice."[86] By 1969, with the help of the act, 61 percent of voting-age blacks were registered to vote, up from an estimated 23 percent prior to that year.

Racism, Police Brutality, and Economic Despair

Because gains such as voting rights and integration of southern schools angered and frustrated many white Americans, violence against blacks and civil rights advocates was common in the 1960s, highlighted by the assassinations of Martin Luther King Jr. in April 1968 and civil rights activist and presidential hopeful Robert F. Kennedy in June 1968.

At the same time, some young blacks got tired of relying solely on peaceful activism. They began advocating Black Power, a movement that emphasized racial pride and relied on violence, if necessary, to achieve political and economic aims. Some young blacks joined groups such as the Black Panthers, whose popularity was based in part on their reputation for confronting police officers. Black militancy coupled with police brutality and economic inequality produced riots in 1966 and 1967 in cities such as Atlanta, San Francisco, Oakland, Cleveland, Chicago, New York, and Detroit. A 1967 *New York Times* editorial read, "This has been America's summer of confrontation. In dozens of communities . . . powerful forces of Negro revolt have lashed out against the established order on a scale and with a fury that are unprecedented."[87]

Eventually the violence eased, although racial inequality, police brutality, and economic despair remained constant conditions in many southern communities and inner-city neighborhoods outside the South. Such conditions fostered interracial tension and other social problems that went almost ignored by the majority of Americans unless some event provoked a public outcry. One of the most high-profile of such cases occurred in 1991 and involved a black man named Rodney King. After a high-speed chase, white Los Angeles police officers brutally beat King when he resisted arrest, and the beating was videotaped by a passerby. Despite the evidence of excessive force, the officers were acquitted of the charges. The news triggered riots in the black community which resulted in more than 50 deaths.

The Long Struggle Continues

In the twenty-first century, undercurrents of racial tension still periodically flare into violence, but blacks have clearly made great progress since the abolition of slavery in 1865. Civil rights guarantees and affirmative action programs have helped many get better educations and better jobs. More blacks are achieving prominence in business, education, government, and other fields than ever before. Oprah Winfrey is the nation's first African American billionaire. Michael Jordan, Magic Johnson, and Bill Cosby are national icons who command widespread respect and admiration. Blacks have served as US secretaries of state, presidents of Ivy League universities, and CEOs of large industrial corporations. Most notably, in 2008 Barack Obama became the first black president of the United States. Among more ordinary black Americans, more than one-quarter work in management, professional, and related occupations. In

Enormous civil rights gains been made in the United States since the abolition of slavery. Possibly the most notable example of the change in American attitudes toward race is the 2008 election of Barack Obama, the first black US president (pictured here in 2012).

2007 there were 1.9 million black-owned businesses in America. Some 1.5 million blacks had received an advanced degree by 2009.

Nevertheless, the legacy of slavery has not been erased. Blacks still lag behind whites economically and socially. Many Americans still privately believe that blacks are an inferior race. Others are convinced that black unemployment, poverty, and criminality stem from stupidity and laziness rather than frustration, hopelessness, and anger. As Eric Foner writes, "No one can argue, at the dawn of the twenty-first century, that America's long struggle with racial inequality has ended or that the contradictions created by the existence of slavery in a country that considers itself an embodiment of freedom have been fully resolved."[88]

There is clearly much work to be done before the conditions of equality dreamed of by William Lloyd Garrison, Frederick Douglass, Martin Luther King Jr., and others are reality. Nevertheless, more black Americans than ever before have faith that their country will one day become the equal-opportunity nation that it ought to be. As King said in 1963,

> With this faith we will be able to hew out of the mountain of despair a stone of hope. With this faith we will be able to transform the jangling discords of our nation into a beautiful symphony of brotherhood. With this faith we will be able to work together, to pray together, to struggle together, to go to jail together, to stand up for freedom together, knowing that we will be free one day.[89]

Source Notes

Introduction: The Defining Characteristics of the Abolition of Slavery

1. William Lloyd Garrison, "Address to the Colonization Society," Document Library, Teaching American History.org, July 4, 1829. www.teachingamericanhistory.org.
2. Garrison, "Address to the Colonization Society."
3. John C. Calhoun, "Slavery a Positive Good," Teaching American History.org, February 6, 1837. www.teachingamericanhistory.org.
4. Quoted in Douglas Harper, "Northern Emancipation," Slavery in the North.com, 2003. www.slavenorth.com.
5. Quoted in Geoffrey C. Ward, Ric Burns, and Ken Burns, *The Civil War: An Illustrated History.* New York: Knopf, 1990, p. 14.
6. Quoted in Ward, Burns, and Burns, *The Civil War*, p. 30.
7. Abraham Lincoln, "Letter to Horace Greeley," Abraham Lincoln Online.org, August 22, 1862. http://showcase.netins.net.
8. Quoted in Ward, Burns, and Burns, *The Civil War*, p. 181.

Chapter One: What Conditions Led to the Abolition of Slavery?

9. Francis Daniel Pastorius et al. "A Minute Against Slavery, address to the Germantown Monthly Meeting," Quaker Heritage Press, 1688. www.qhpress.org.
10. Benjamin Franklin, "Petition from the Pennsylvania Society for the Abolition of Slavery," Historic Documents, February 3, 1790. www.ushistory.org.
11. National Archives, "The Declaration of Independence," July 4, 1776. www.archives.gov.
12. Quoted in Steven Mintz, "The Constitution and Slavery," Digital History, 2007. www.digitalhistory.uh.edu.

13. Thomas Jefferson, "Wolf by the Ears," Jefferson Monticello Web Site, April 22, 1820. www.monticello.org.

14. Quoted in Ward, Burns, and Burns, *The Civil War*, p. 12.

15. Thomas Jefferson, "The Kentucky Resolutions of 1878," Constitution Society, November 10, 1798. www.constitution.org.

16. Calhoun, "Slavery a Positive Good."

17. Calhoun, "Slavery a Positive Good."

18. William G. Elliot, *The Story of Archer Alexander. From Slavery to Freedom.* Boston: Cupples, Upham, 1885, p. 18; online edition, Documenting the American South, 2004. http://docsouth.unc.edu.

19. Quoted in Jean M. West, "King Cotton; The Fiber of Slavery," Slavery in America, 2012. www.slaveryinamerica.org.

20. Quoted in Clayton J. Butler, "The African-American Experience: From Slavery to Emancipation," Civil War Trust, 2011. www.civilwar.org.

21. William Moore, "Ex-Slave Stories," Civil War Home Page, 2011. www.civil-war.net.

22. Sarah Frances Shaw Graves, "Still Carries Scars from Lashes," Civil War Home Page, 2011. www.civil-war.net.

23. Quoted in Ward, Burns, and Burns, *The Civil War*, p. 9.

24. Quoted in Ward, Burns, and Burns, *The Civil War*, p. 9.

25. Quoted in Harriet Beecher Stowe, "Uncle Tom's Cabin, 1852," chap. 7 in *The Life of Harriet Beecher Stowe*, University of Michigan Library, January 1, 1891.

26. Quoted in Stowe, *Uncle Tom's Cabin*, p. xxxvii.

Chapter Two: Slavery Divides the Nation

27. Abraham Lincoln, "Lincoln's House Divided Speech," Historic Documents, June 16, 1858. www.ushistory.org.

28. Quoted in PBS, "Historical Document, Missouri Compromise 1820," *Africans in America*, 1999. www.pbs.org.

29. Quoted in The Slave Heritage Resource Center, "The Missouri Compromise," 2003. www.sonofthesouth.net.

30. Quoted in The Slave Heritage Resource Center, "The Missouri Compromise."

31. Quoted in United States Senate, "Bitter Feelings in the Senate Chamber," April 3, 1850. www.senate.gov.

32. News in History.Com, "Workings of the Fugitive Slave Law," *Milwaukee Sentinel*, October 25, 1850. www.newsinhistory.com.

33. Henry Brown, *Narrative of the Life of Henry Box Brown, Written by Himself*. Manchester: Lee & Glynn, 1851, p. 57, online edition, Documenting the American South, 2004. http://docsouth.unc.edu.

34. Good Reads.com, "Harriet Tubman Quotes," 2012. www.goodreads.com.

35. Quoted in Ward, Burns, and Burns, *The Civil War*, p. 20.

36. Quoted in Allan Nevins, *Ordeal of the Union: A House Dividing 1852–1857*. New York: Scribner's and Sons, 1947, pp. 111–112.

37. Quoted in Ward, Burns, and Burns, *The Civil War*, p. 21.

38. Quoted in Philip R. Devlin, "John Brown and the Civil War: The Connecticut Connection," *East Hampton-Portland (CT) Patch*, May 10, 2011. http://easthampton-ct.patch.com.

39. Quoted in Ward, Burns, and Burns, *The Civil War*, p. 4.

40. Quoted in Ward, Burns, and Burns, *The Civil War*, p. 6.

41. *Charleston Mercury*, "What Shall the South Carolina Legislature Do?" Editorials on Secession Project, November 3, 1860. www.historians.org.

Chapter Three: Slavery Leads to War

42. Abraham Lincoln, "Speech at Chicago, Illinois," Teaching American History. org, July 10, 1858. www.teachingamericanhistory.org.

43. Quoted in *New York Times*, "Newspaper Reports: South Carolina. The Minute Men of Charleston. The Harpers' Periodicals Proscribed,." November 5, 1860. www.nytimes.com.

44. Abraham Lincoln, "First Inaugural Address." www.ushistory.org.

45. Lincoln, "First Inaugural Address."

46. Abraham Lincoln, "Proclamation by the President; Seventy-five Thousand Volunteers and an Extra Session of Congress. By the President of the United States. A Proclamation," *New York Times*, April 15, 1861. www.nytimes.com.

47. Quoted in Ward, Burns, and Burns, *The Civil War*, p. 178.

48. Quoted in Dick Nolan, *Benjamin Franklin Butler, the Damnedest Yankee*. Novato, CA: Presidio, 1991, pp.101–102.

49. Quoted in James M. McPherson, *The Struggle for Equality*, Princeton, NJ: Princeton University Press, 1992, p. 93.

50. Quoted in Ward, Burns, and Burns, *The Civil War*, p. 246.

51. Quoted in Mr. Lincoln and Freedom, "Compensated Emancipation," 2012. www.mrlincolnandfreedom.org.

52. Frederick Douglass, *Frederick Douglass: Autobiographies; Narrative of the Life of Frederick Douglass, an American Slave; My Bondage and My Freedom; Life and Times of Frederick Douglass*, Henry Louis Gates Jr., ed. New York: Library of America, 1994, p. 792.

53. Quoted in The War for States' Rights, "Emancipation Proclamation 'The Southern Reaction,'" 2012. http://civilwar.bluegrass.net.

54. Quoted in Mr. Lincoln and Freedom, "International Reaction," 2012. www.mrlincolnandfreedom.org.

55. Douglass, *Frederick Douglass: Autobiographies,* pp. 791–92.

56. Quoted in My Growth Plan. org, "Booker T. Washington," 2011. www.mygrowthplan.org.

57. Quoted in American Civil War.com, "History of Colored Troops in the American Civil War," 2011. http://americancivilwar.com.

58. Quoted in EyeWitness to History, "The Civil War Ends—a Small Town's Reaction, 1865," 2004. www.eyewitnesstohistory.com.

59. Mary Boykin Chesnut, *A Diary from Dixie, as Written by Mary Boykin Chesnut*, Isabella D. Martin and Myrta Lockett Avary, eds. New York: D. Appleton, 1905, p. 387, online edition, Documenting the American South, 2004. http://docsouth.unc.edu.

60. Fountain Hughes, "Personal Narratives," *Slavery and the Making of America*, PBS, 2004. www.pbs.org.

61. United States Constitution, "Amendment Thirteen—Slavery Abolished," December 6, 1865. www.usconstitution.net.

62. Quoted in Sandra Thomas, "Life After the Thirteenth Amendment," University of Rochester, 2012. www.history.rochester.edu.

Chapter Four: Free but Unequal

63. Steven Mintz, "America's Reconstruction: Introduction," Digital History, 2007. www.digitalhistory.uh.edu.

64. Quoted in Ward, Burns, and Burns, *The Civil War*, p. 360.

65. Quoted in Tom Head, "The 8 Worst Presidents Ever," About.com, 2012. http://civilliberty.about.com.

66. George Washington University, "Ordinances of the Convention—Arkansas Black Codes," February 6, 1867. http://home.gwu.edu.

67. Quoted in David Wiegand, "Black History: Reconstruction," Bilerico Project, 2011. www.bilerico.com.

68. Quoted in Ellis Paxon Oberholtzer, *A History of the United States Since the Civil War, 1865–1868*. New York: Macmillan, 1917, p. 137.

69. Charles Sumner "A Bridge from Slavery to Freedom," speech, US Senate, June 13 and 15, 1864, *Slavery and the Making of America*, PBS. www.pbs.org.

70. Beverly Wilson Palmer and Holly Byers Ochoa, eds., *The Selected Papers of Thaddeus Stevens*, vol. 2, April 1865–August 1868. Pittsburgh, PA: University of Pittsburgh Press, 1998, p. 198.

71. U.S. Constitution online, "Amendment 15—Race No Bar to Vote," February 3, 1870. www.usconstitution.net.

72. Quoted in Eric Foner, *Forever Free: The Story of Emancipation and Reconstruction*. New York: Knopf, 2005, p. 148.

73. John Roy Lynch, *The Facts of Reconstruction*. New York: Neale, 1913, p. 44.

74. University of Missouri-Kansas City School of Law, "Proceedings of the Senate Sitting for the Trial of Andrew Johnson, President of the United States," Famous Trials, March 4, 1868. http://law2.umkc.edu.

75. Quoted in *Harper's Weekly*, "The Impeachment of Andrew Johnson," June 6, 1868. www.andrewjohnson.com.

76. Quoted in EyeWitness to History, "The Ku Klux Klan, 1868," 2006. www.eyewitnesstohistory.com.

77. Foner, *Forever Free*, p. 213.

Chapter Five: What Is the Legacy of the Abolition of Slavery?

78. Center for History and New Media, "The Civil Rights Act of March 1, 1875," 2012. http://chnm.gmu.edu.

79. The History of Jim Crow, "Eyewitness to Jim Crow; Willie Wallace Remembers," 2011. www.jimcrowhistory.org.

80. Quoted in William Bradford Huie, "The Shocking Story of Approved Killing in Mississippi," PBS, January 24, 1956. www.pbs .org.

81. Ronald L.F. Davis, "Surviving Jim Crow: In-Depth Essay," The History of Jim Crow, 2011. www.jimcrowhistory.org.

82. Quoted in Ken Hare, "Overview," The Story of the Montgomery Bus Boycott, 1955–1956. www.montgomeryboycott.com.

83. Martin Luther King Jr., "Statement on Ending the Bus Boycott," Martin Luther King Jr. Research and Education Institute, December 20, 1956. http://mlk-kpp01.stanford.edu.

84. Martin Luther King Jr., "Address to First Montgomery Improvement Association (MIA) Mass Meeting, at Holt Street Baptist Church," Martin Luther King Jr. Research and Education Institute, December 5, 1955. http://mlk-kpp01.stanford.edu.

85. Martin Luther King Jr., "Our God Is Marching On," Famous Speeches and Speech Topics, March 21, 1965. www.famous-speeches-and-speech-topics.info.

86. Lyndon B. Johnson, "Lyndon B. Johnson; Voting Rights Address," Great American Documents, March 15, 1965. www.greatamerican documents.com.

87. *New York Times*, "Editorial: The Responsibility; White and Black," July 30, 1967. www.pbs.org.

88. Foner, *Forever Free*, p. xix.

89. Martin Luther King Jr., "I Have a Dream Speech," Historic Documents, August 28, 1963. www.ushistory.org.

Important People During the
Abolition of Slavery

Henry Ward Beecher: A prominent American clergyman, social reformer, and abolitionist. In the 1830s he raised funds to buy weapons for those willing to oppose slavery in Kansas, and during the Civil War his church raised and equipped a volunteer infantry regiment.

John Brown: A revolutionary and controversial abolitionist who advocated and practiced armed insurrection as a means to abolish slavery. After leading murderous raids against proslavery adherents in Kansas and Virginia, he was captured, tried, and hung for his crimes.

Frederick Douglass: An American writer, speaker, and former slave who, after escaping from his master in 1838, became one of the leaders of the abolitionist movement. Because he was so polished, he stood as a living example of the falseness of slaveholders' arguments that slaves did not have the intellectual capacity to function as independent citizens.

William Lloyd Garrison: A prominent American journalist, social reformer, and abolitionist. He is best known as the editor of the abolitionist newspaper the *Liberator* and as one of the founders of the American Anti-Slavery Society.

John Jay: An American politician, statesman, and one of the Founding Fathers of the United States. He was founder and president of the New York Manumission Society, which organized boycotts against newspapers and merchants involved in the slave trade.

Andrew Johnson: Succeeded Abraham Lincoln as president in 1865 following the latter's assassination. Johnson then presided over the contentious Reconstruction era that followed the Civil War. His Reconstruction policies failed to promote the rights of freed slaves, and he came under political attack from Radical Republicans.

Martin Luther King Jr.: An American clergyman, activist, and prominent leader in the civil rights movement of the 1960s. He became known for his nonviolent methods of protest, and in 1964 he became the youngest person to receive the Nobel Peace Prize for his work to end racial segregation and discrimination.

Abraham Lincoln: The sixteenth president of the United States, serving from March 1861 until his assassination in April 1865. He successfully led his country through the Civil War in which he preserved the Union and ended slavery.

Rosa Parks: A black American civil rights activist. Her refusal to give up her bus seat to make room for a white passenger sparked the Montgomery Bus Boycott in 1955. Her act of defiance became an important symbol of the modern civil rights movement, and Parks became an international symbol of resistance to segregation.

Harriet Beecher Stowe: An American author and abolitionist. She was sister to Henry Ward Beecher. Stowe's 1852 novel *Uncle Tom's Cabin* energized antislavery forces in the American North, but provoked widespread anger in the South.

Charles Sumner: An American politician and senator from Massachusetts. He was the leader of the antislavery forces in Massachusetts and in 1856 was nearly killed on the Senate floor by Congressman Preston Brooks for his antislavery remarks. A leader of the Radical Republicans during the Reconstruction era, he fought hard to provide equal civil and voting rights for freedmen.

Harriet Tubman: A black American abolitionist, humanitarian, and Union spy during the Civil War. After escaping from slavery in 1849, she made 13 missions to rescue more than 70 slaves, using the network of antislavery activists and safe houses known as the Underground Railroad. She was the first woman to lead an armed expedition in the war, guiding a raid which freed more than 700 slaves in South Carolina.

Booker T. Washington: An American author, speaker, former slave, and one of the best-known figures in the black community from 1890 to 1915. He founded the Tuskegee Institute in Alabama in 1881, then went on to gain the support of wealthy philanthropists whose funds helped construct and operate more than 5,000 schools for blacks throughout the South in the late nineteenth and early twentieth centuries.

For Further Research

Books

Judith Bloom Fradin and Dennis Brindell Fradin, *Stolen into Slavery: The True Story of Solomon Northup, Free Black Man*. Washington, DC: National Geographic Society, 2012.

Archibald Henry Grimké, *William Lloyd Garrison: The Abolitionist*. (Reprint.) UK: Cambridge University Press, 2010.

Tony Horwitz, *Midnight Rising: John Brown and the Raid That Sparked the Civil War*. New York: Henry Holt, 2011.

Owen W. Muelder, *Theodore Dwight Weld and the American Anti-Slavery Society*. Jefferson, NC: McFarland, 2011.

Linda Barrett Osborne, *Miles to Go for Freedom: Segregation and Civil Rights in the Jim Crow Years*. New York: Abrams, 2012.

Joan Potter, *African-American Firsts: Famous Little-Known and Unsung Triumphs of Blacks in America*. New York: Kensington, 2002.

David S. Reynolds, *Mightier than the Sword:* Uncle Tom's Cabin *and the Battle for America*. New York: W. W. Norton, 2011.

Websites

Aboard the Underground Railroad (www.nps.gov/nr/travel/under ground). Information on Underground Railroad including maps and historic places that can be visited.

The African-American Mosaic (www.loc.gov/exhibits/african). The Library of Congress resource guide for the study of black history and culture. Includes information on abolition and ex-slave narratives.

Africans in America (www.pbs.org/wgbh/aia/home.html). America's journey through slavery is presented. Includes a valuable resource bank, youth activity guide, and teachers' guide.

American Abolitionism (americanabolitionist.liberalarts.iupui.edu). A site for those who are interested in studying one of the most important reform movements in US history.

Civil Rights Movement Veterans (www.crmvet.org). Veterans of the 1960s civil rights movement tell their stories. The website includes photos, documents, a timeline, and more.

Civil War (www.civilwar.com). An extensive guide to the Civil War. The section on slavery covers the history of slavery, slavery and the Union, and African American soldiers.

The History of Jim Crow (www.jimcrowhistory.org/history/history .htm). Includes in-depth essays, narratives, and lesson plans about the Jim Crow era in the United States.

We Shall Overcome (www.nps.gov/nr/travel/civilrights). For those who would like to visit important sites of the civil rights movement, this website includes maps and other information.

Index

Note: Boldface page numbers indicate illustrations.

Picture Credits

Cover: © Thinkstock

© adoc-photos/Corbis: 9

AP Images: 72, 79

Art Resource, NY: 32, 36, 63

© Bettmann/Corbis: 21, 55, 77

© Corbis: 24, 49

North Wind Picture Archives: 16, 46

Thinkstock: 6, 7

Steve Zmina: 12, 35

About the Author

Diane Yancey is a freelance author who lives in the Pacific Northwest. She published her first book in 1989 and has written four other books on the Civil War era including *Civil War Generals of the Union*, *Leaders and Generals of the North and South*, *Strategic Battles of the Civil War*, and *Frederick Douglass*.